the audacity of preaching

the audacity of preaching

THE LYMAN BEECHER LECTURES

YALE DIVINITY SCHOOL 1961

Gene E. Bartlett

HARPER & BROTHERS
PUBLISHERS, NEW-YORK

Grateful acknowledgment is made to the following for permission to reprint portions of the works indicated:

Brandt & Brandt: *John Brown's Body* by Stephen Vincent Benét (New York: Holt, Rinehart and Winston; copyright 1927, 1928 by Stephen Vincent Benét, copyright renewed 1955, 1956 by Rosemary Carr Benét).

The Macmillan Company, New York: Dietrich Bonhoeffer, *The Cost of Discipleship* (copyright © 1959 by SCM Press Ltd.).

Holt, Rinehart & Winston, Inc., New York: Stephen Vincent Benét, *Western Star* (copyright 1943 by Farrar & Rinehart, Inc.).

To my wife

Jean Kenyon Bartlett

and to our children

David
Marion
Randall
Stephen
Margaret

... caught up into love, and taught the whole
Of life in a new rhythm.

—*Elizabeth Barrett Browning*
SONNETS FROM THE PORTUGUESE, VII

CONTENTS

PREFACE A WORD ABOUT VIEWPOINT 11

ACKNOWLEDGMENTS 13

CHAPTER ONE THE CLAIM: INCREDI-
BLE, BUT INESCAPABLE 17

    I. OUR SEARCH FOR IDENTITY 18

    II. INCOMPLETE IDENTITIES 20

    III. THE REAL GROUND OF PREACHING 22

    IV. PART OF THE EVENT 25

    V. THE SECULAR BARRIER 31

    VI. THE PREACHER'S REAL
    ENGAGEMENT 35

CHAPTER TWO THE SERMON: SOME-
THING OUT OF THE ORDINARY 37

    I. BELIEF: THE GREAT EXPECTANCY 39

    II. REMEMBRANCE: RECALLING WHAT
    GOD HAS DONE 41

    III. THE PEW: AN EXPOSED POSITION 42

7

Contents

IV. THE WORD: ELEMENTS OF AN ART   50

V.   LOVE: THE GREATEST OF THESE   59

VI. CONCLUSION   59

CHAPTER THREE THE PASTORATE: INVOLVED FOR LIFE   61

I.   A LIFE OF DISTRACTION AND
      DILUTION?   62

II.   THE SCHOLARSHIP OF INVOLVE-
      MENT   66

III. DIALOGUE WITH LIFE   71

IV.   THE LIVING AUTHORITY   74

V.   MAKING THE CHURCH VITAL   77

VI.   ENDING UP IN DEBT   81

CHAPTER FOUR THE WORLD: THIS WAY TO LIFE   82

I.   WHICH WAY TO LIFE?   84

II.   INVITATION TO FULFILLMENT   92

III. WHAT PASTORAL PREACHING
      REQUIRES   99

IV.   BEYOND ALL THAT WE ASK OR
      THINK   104

Contents

CHAPTER FIVE **THE IMPERATIVE:**
WHERE THE KINGDOM AND THE
CULTURE MEET   105

    I.   THE THRUST FOR RIGHTEOUSNESS   107

    II. APPOINTMENT WITH DESPAIR   108

    III. THE IMPERATIVES OF MATURITY   110

    IV. THE PASTORAL PROPHET   123

    V.   URGENT—APPLY LOCALLY   126

CHAPTER SIX **THE CALLING:** *MATURING*
IN THE MINISTRY   128

    I.   FACING THE FUNDAMENTAL
        ALARM   130

    II. SOURCES OF PERSONAL RENEWAL   135

    III. KEEPING RELATIONSHIPS REAL   146

    IV. TO WHOM DOES THE MINISTER
        BELONG?   150

NOTES   153

BIBLICAL REFERENCES   156

INDEX   157

PREFACE

A WORD ABOUT VIEWPOINT

THERE IS A FUNDAMENTAL HONESTY ABOUT OUR
common word "viewpoint." In itself it is a confession that
what any man sees of reality is determined in part by the
point from which he views it. "Every man sees what he takes
with him," said Goethe, and it is a fact which must be taken
into account in weighing any word.

At the outset, therefore, it will help to make explicit what
soon will be apparent, namely, that the viewpoint of these
lectures throughout is the Christian pastorate. It could not be
otherwise, for this is where my experience has been. Yet this
imposes no confinement, but indeed offers a genuine sense of
freedom. There seems to be an important point in the preparation of lectures like these. It may be called the release of
despair. It is that hour in which a man at last gives up trying
to fashion timeless Beecher Lectures, with all the name implies,
and settles instead for trying to say something which is real and
faithful to his deepest experience. That release I have accepted, for better or for worse, and shall consider the meaning
of preaching almost wholly in the context of the average
pastorate.

Yet this is far more than any man's concern. In recent years it has emerged as an urgent matter for the whole church. For serious questions have arisen about the contemporary pastorate: Can it be real? Is the minister sentenced in it to a life of distraction and dilution? Has it become so organized and structured that it requires an organization man more than a man of God? Is the acceptance of a pastorate the death sentence for scholarly interests? There seems no escape from facing these questions now often weighing upon men long in the pastorate, and equally confronting the theological student who, wanting to be a pastor, yet wonders whether it is really possible in the deepest sense of the word.

So these lectures represent a viewpoint that I have sought to put under the severest scrutiny of which I am capable. In the hope that they may contribute to the conversation now current about the meaning and nature of the pastorate, they reflect pastoral experience as honestly examined and faithfully reported as possible.

Certain convictions will show through again and again: that the pastorate does represent the point at which the gospel really engages life, that even in the contemporary church there is sufficient freedom open to the minister who wants to make his pastoral relations real, that the hope for finding reality is not so much in rearranging external things imposed upon us by our culture, but in the reacceptance of new meanings which must rest in the minister himself, that in terms of conditions for a lifelong learning the pastorate offers a living, even exciting, option, that the insistence upon the depth dimension will find ready response and support in most congregations. These are facets of a central belief which permeates these chapters.

Whether this is merely the prejudice of one who seeks to justify himself, or a measured and weighed viewpoint which really looks at truth, you must judge. And I am sure you will!

ACKNOWLEDGMENTS

THROUGH THESE DAYS OF preparation I have been reminded again and again of my debt beyond paying to all those who have given me the understanding, the insights, and the knowledge which make the ministry possible. I wish I could acknowledge fully those who have contributed so much. But in the nature of human relationships many of these influences have become so much a part of my life that it is quite impossible to identify them. Who can say how many influences there are in one's life which are forgotten but not gone?

Yet some indebtedness is very clear. Now I know why every Beecher lecturer has expressed his genuine appreciation to the whole community at Yale. Dean Liston Pope, the members of the faculty and student body, and the ministers who returned for the lectures made a formidable responsibility an occasion to be remembered for its warmth and response. When the invitation first came I wondered why they ever asked me. Before I was through the preparation I wondered why I ever accepted! It is more than possible that those who heard the lectures wondered both! But I shall remember through the years the genuine welcome of Dean Pope and the Yale community.

Acknowledgments

From the standpoint of the lectures there was a very fortunate coincidence in an invitation extended to me by the American Association of Theological Schools. Though they did not know that I was engaged in study for the Beecher Lectures, they invited me to share in four two-day seminars on preaching being conducted by the AATS for teachers of preaching across the country. These seminars, made possible by a grant of the Lilly Foundation, offered conversations with teachers of preaching in about fifty of our theological schools. This experience coming in the year of preparation for the lectures gave me many opportunities to raise some of the questions and try out some of the ideas which are on these pages. I am grateful to the AATS for their invitation, more timely than they knew, and to those able professors of homiletics gathered in Berkeley, Chicago, St. Paul, and Dallas who made the conversations on contemporary preaching so stimulating.

There are some persons to whom I owe special acknowledgment. Dr. C. E. Lemmon, pastor of the First Christian Church of Columbia, Missouri, a personal friend of many years, is a special student of the Beecher Lectures and I turned to him in trying to find the emphasis which would fit best into the series which covers so many years.

One of my greatest debts is to Miss Blanche Larson, my assistant and secretary in the First Baptist Church of Los Angeles, who brought to the preparation of the original manuscript such a contagious interest and unfailing enthusiasm that she went far beyond the call of duty. The depth of her interest was such that the whole church recognized it and sent her across the continent to be at Yale for the convocation. To this recognition by the church I add my profound gratitude.

In similar way, the revision and final preparation of these pages was carried out with great efficiency by my secretary at Colgate Rochester, Miss Marjorie Ewell, and on occasion by

14

Acknowledgments

Mrs. Kenneth Hicks who assisted her. I express my deep thanks to Miss Ewell for seeing these pages through the laborious details which publication requires.

To these must be added my abiding gratitude to those congregations who gave me the opportunity to be their preacher. I remember them with such warmth and affection. They are reflected in these pages for they taught me that preaching indeed is the act of the whole church. It was their expectancy and their trust which made preaching so real and exciting a part of my ministry. To the congregations of the Baptist Church in Hilton, New York, Calvary Baptist in Syracuse, New York, First Baptist in Columbia, Missouri, First Baptist in Evanston, Illinois, and the First Baptist of Los Angeles, California, I can only say, with Paul, "I thank my God in all remembrance of you . . . thankful for your partnership in the gospel from the first day until now."

GENE E. BARTLETT

January, 1962
Colgate Rochester Divinity School

CHAPTER ONE

The Claim:

INCREDIBLE, BUT
INESCAPABLE

RECENTLY THERE CAME TO MY ATTENTION A
letter which sounded a contemporary note. Written by a man
engaged in active pulpit ministry, it included this observation: "All I can say and feel is, that by the change of times
the pulpit has lost its place. It does only part of that whole
which used to be done by it alone. Once it was newspaper,
schoolmaster, theological treatise, a stimulant to good works.
. . . Now these are partitioned out to different offices, and the
pulpit is no more the pulpit of three centuries back, than the
authority of a householder is that of Abraham."[1]

Surely we will recognize a contemporary complaint in these
words. Yet it is significant to note that they were written in
July, 1851, and the writer was none other than Frederick W.
Robertson. The question was in his own mind at the very time
when he was writing a chapter in the history of preaching which
we count superlative.

In every generation the preacher seems to have struggled with
his own experience of "the fall"—the sense that in his day
preaching is not what it once was. Certainly that idea moves

among us with the greatest of ease. It is part of the state of mind which has caused some to designate the ministry as "the perplexed profession."

I. Our Search for Identity

Why not? Who could face the claim and not feel the tension between preaching as it is meant to be and preaching as it usually is. Even to the preacher his claim is touched with audacity. When we see it to the full, we know that in our culture no other makes a profession to compare with it. The scientist makes an amazing claim. He holds that by limiting the area of his investigation and submitting himself to the discipline of the scientific method, he can come to a pragmatic knowledge of an area of reality. Our scientific age is clear evidence that he has fulfilled his claim to an amazing degree.

There are other claims in our culture. The artist affirms that by developing his sensitivity he can perceive the essential meaning of an area of beauty, put it into an art form, and impart it to others. Our impressive heritage of art in many forms is evidence that he, too, has made good on his claim.

The writer, working with words, has another assumption. He believes that he can translate experience to the written word and release it again to those who read. Joseph Conrad said of himself, "My task which I am trying to achieve is, by the power of the written word to make you hear, to make you feel—it is, before all, to make you *see*. That—and no more, and it is everything."[2] Our libraries are tangible witness that the writer's claim often is fulfilled.

But beside the preacher's claim, all others seem restricted and partial. Consider what he affirms when he comes to his pulpit to preach! By the very act he is asserting that he can enter into the knowledge, not of a limited area of reality, but of God, the ground of all reality. Preaching with all its variations ultimately must rest upon the claim that we can know what God is and what by His help man may become. In short, the preacher claims to know the will and Word of God, and to proclaim it in relation to the options and situations of his time. Is there any claim quite so audacious? Is it any wonder that we fall so far short?

After Thomas Wolfe's tragically early death, there were found among his papers plans and plots for more books than any man could possibly write. Considering all that he had laid out for himself, one of his biographers says, "The error was not in discipline or in planning, it was in the scope of the design itself, too great and too unmanageable to be realized in one lifetime."[3]

Perhaps in part it is the sheer "scope of the design" which has raised again the question of the preacher's identity. Essentially, the search for meaning in preaching centers in a few basic questions which, like the notes in the musical scale, appear again and again in changing combinations. Sometimes one question is dominant, sometimes another. There is the query, What shall we preach? Or again, How shall we preach it? Equally, in our time we have asked, To whom do we preach? But included in that basic scale of questions is another which for a time has come to be dominant for us. It is the searching one, Who is the preacher?

In one way this is a question with unhealthy tendencies. We lose much of the vitality of preaching if we become engaged in a kind of progressive self-absorption. Subjective questions are always dangerous, and increasingly demanding. If we turn only inward to find our identity, we stand to lose an undefinable power in preaching. On the other hand, if the need for identity turns us outward to find ourselves in the whole scheme of Christian thought, then it is a healthy query, full of promise.

The only answer to our search is in our recovered relationship to the whole *gestalt* of Christian history and belief.

II. Incomplete Identities

Yet our need is urgent and we are tempted to accept partial answers. The very word "identity," which expresses what we are seeking, connotes relationship. So if you ask a man for an identification, he will give you his name which relates him to a family. He will also give his address which relates him to a community. He may even add his citizenship and his vocation which relate him to a nation and a profession respectively. We are known, you see, by the company we keep!

Recognizing this, we need to ask: In what relationship then does the preacher find his true identity? With what is he identified which gives him his distinction in calling and claim? This seems to be a part of our perplexity. Carl Sandburg tells of the chameleon who got along very well adjusting moment by moment to his environment until one day he had to cross a Scotch plaid. It is related that he died at the crossroads, heroically trying to relate to everything at once!

In our search for identity as preachers we seem to have moved in several directions. Some have tried to find it in the *institutional* relationship. In a day when we have recovered with urgency and no little excitement the sense of the historic Christian community of believers, some ministers have found their identity as servants of that community as it comes to visible form in the church institution. To build the church, to guide it, and to impart to future generations a strong working community—this is the business of preaching as some would see it.

Many contemporary ministers have turned to the *psychological* relationship. Strongly influenced by the counseling movement, they understand their preaching essentially as a pastoral relation to people. In the pulpit as well as in the study, as they see it, a man is engaged in a personal encounter which helps people feel accepted and understood. In the preaching relationship he hopes to be a counselor and even on occasion a therapist. It is as an arm of pastoral outreach that preaching for them has its significance.

At the same time, there are other preachers who turn to the *liturgical* relationship for their identity. The pulpit has its significance for them because it is related to the altar. They recognize the clear truth in the words of the late Dean Sperry, "The conduct of public worship is the original office of a church and remains always its distinctive office. . . . No other service which it renders society can compare in importance with this."[4] Putting this truth in first place, some preachers know themselves primarily as priests in the pulpit as well as at the altar.

Again, there are preachers who would turn to the *cultural* relationship for the meaning of their ministry. They affirm the priority of moral and spiritual values. Where such values are present, the preacher must conserve them; where they are absent, he must seek reform to bring them about. His work as preacher is to be leaven and light in our culture, and partner with those humane influences which bring health to a society. He would not like to live in a community where there is no church, and of course, no preacher!

Again, it is clear that for some ministers the *subjective* relationship is sufficient. Their identity rests upon the reality of their inner call. They lift to prime importance the affirmation of Calvin that "the secret call is the honest testimony of the heart that we accept the office." Could a man ask for more than that?

These are relationships in which we have sought to find ourselves and the very words we use for the minister reflect their historic character. We call him churchman, pastor, priest, parson, man of God, or divine, each reflecting the very identities we have mentioned. They have become a part of our language. Is any of them sufficient? Or are they only incomplete identities? All of them have truth, that is obvious. But is any the central truth? Or do we still need to find the fundamental ground of the preacher's task, upon which these others rest?

III. *The Real Ground of Preaching*

To find that deeper answer we must turn in the one direction in which authority lies, namely, to the Bible witness. We who are in the historic Christian tradition can rest our case on no other foundation than the Biblical Word.

Even a preliminary search suggests the answer which deeper study corroborates. The note is sounded in the very first words, "In the beginning God." The sacred history which follows again and again proclaims that God *made Himself known* to His people. From the first traditional stories of faith which tell what God did, to the towering words of the prophets which relate what God said, there is a recurring theme of God's impelling and gracious initiative. It is made to sing in the affirmation of the Psalmist, "Bless the Lord, O my soul, and forget not all *his* benefits: who forgives . . . heals . . . redeems . . . crowns . . . satisfies." It continues in the narratives of the New Testament which always speak of God's in-breaking: "And the glory of the Lord shone round about them." It is the awesome meaning of the witness in the letters of Paul: "God was in Christ, reconciling the world." Even the closing apocalyptic passages reflect it: "I saw a new heaven and a new earth . . . coming down out of heaven from God."

There it is, then, like the recurring theme of a symphony with infinite variations. But always it is there: God's prior action in all things. We know Him because He first willed to make

Himself known. We love Him because He first loved us. We have heard because He has spoken. We are reconciled because He offered reconciliation. We are found because He sought.

Here we stand at the ground of preaching, so inescapably and audaciously theological. In other words, we cannot answer the question, Who is the preacher? until we first have considered the prior questions, Who is God? How does He work among us? How do we know His will? Only when we have faced these can we move on to ask, Who is the preacher? For only in relationship to the nature of God does the preacher find his own significance and calling. The ground of the preacher's claim is the belief in the continuous self-disclosure of God, His self-giving. As Kingsley once put it, "I believe no man can see the truth of a thing unless God shows it to him."[5] Preaching is an act of faith that God has willed to show that truth, and does it when men offer themselves to speak and to hear.

Many years ago Professor Bruce of Glasgow University, visiting in this country, heard Phillips Brooks preach on three occasions. The impression upon him was so great that he immediately wrote back to Scotland about the experience. Fortunately, the letter has been preserved, and we have his comparison of Brooks to other preachers. He summed it up in these words: "Most preachers take to the pulpit a bucketful or half full of the word of God and pump it out to the congregation; but this man is a great watermain, attached to the everlasting reservoir of truth, and a stream of life pours through him by heavenly gravitation to refresh weary souls."[6]

What a tremendous description of real preaching! It not only describes Brooks as a preacher and his effect upon those who heard him, it also states in vivid imagery the faith upon which preaching rests. It is the conviction that there is a "heavenly gravitation," as Professor Bruce put it by which "a stream of life pours . . . to refresh weary souls." Without that divine gravitation preaching indeed would be foolishness, not saving foolishness, just foolishness, our most prideful pretension.

In this we are affirming that the belief in preaching and the belief in revelation are inextricably tied together. The very term "revelation" connotes self-giving, the initiative of God to make Himself known. Every time we preach we are acting upon that belief.

It seems to me we find support for preaching even in that which classically has been called *the general revelation*. To be sure, in itself that is not enough, but it is a foundation and a foreshadowing of more specific Christian experience. Even that which we know of God through His creation evokes our faith that He has willed to make Himself known. He has spoken of Himself in the order of our universe, reaching from the infinite to the infinitesimal; in the beauty which is spread in such prodigal fashion throughout our world; in the seemingly inexhaustible flow of energy upon which all of us are pensioners even for the day's strength. These speak to us in a preliminary way of God who does not withhold Himself, but gives with unfailing constancy and proclaims His presence in a language meant to be understood. Often He reveals Himself in common human experience. The evidence of His moving among us is seen in the quickening conscience of a man which causes him at times to rebel when other men conform, or to conform to a higher law when other men rebel. Others know Him with unshakeable certainty in the mystic moments which are given to them.

All of these together speak to us of God who is not hidden but disclosed. It gives support to that faith once expressed by A. J. Gossip in words vivid and full of color. "Oh! we shall get our chance. For God is far more eager over it than we are. . . . Always we are surrounded by a persistency of grace which, like the sea on the Dutch dikes, keeps feeling and looking for an opening into our lives, and if it finds even the smallest one . . . at last pours in."[7]

But where does preaching fit into all this? For the moment we are affirming only that when we come to the audacity of preaching, it is grounded in faith that we are not seeking to wrest from a reluctant God knowledge of Himself He has not willed to give. His Word already has gone out to the ends of the earth. Preaching knows that the winds of God blow where they will, but it affirms with confidence their certainty. Marcus Dods once said, "Seamen cannot raise the wind or direct its course, but they can put themselves in the way of the great regular winds."[8] So even our belief in a general revelation gives this much ground for preaching.

IV. *Part of the Event*

But for the Christian preacher it is only the ground, not the specific point of his standing. We are what we are as a people because we believe there has been the special consummate revelation in the event of Jesus Christ. It is in relation to that mighty act of God that we find our identity as Christian preachers and pastors. As the writer of Hebrews stated, "In many and various ways God spoke of old to our fathers by the prophets; but in these last days he has spoken to us by a Son. . . ." We are caught up in that ongoing Event. For in Christ something has happened which is the consummation of all that had gone before, and the illumination of all that is to come. Preaching is rooted in the faith—and this is the audacity—that this Event has never ended. Where the word of Christ is preached, the work of Christ goes on. As Brunner put it, "Faith in Christ is not an interpretation of the word, but it is participation in an event, in something which has happened, which is happening, and which is going to happen."[9]

But what was this Event? Why do we look to it as God's most

wondrous disclosure of Himself? What is the power that emanates from this act of God?

Feeling the limitation of language, we seek for parables. There is such a parable, it seems to me, in a book written some years ago by Admiral Richard E. Byrd entitled *Alone*. It relates his experiences while living in isolation in the Antarctic about one hundred and twenty-three miles from the base camp of Little America. Byrd wanted to gather some scientific data near the Pole. Because it was a hazardous assignment he would not give it to another man but kept it for himself.

The men took him by tractor to the advance post, cut into the ice, and built him a cabin below the surface. There he lived alone for three months, making his observations, and keeping in daily radio contact with Little America. Then something happened which changed the whole situation. He was overcome by carbon monoxide gas and lay on his cot desperately ill, still trying to keep himself alive and in touch with Little America, lest suspecting his plight they set out on a foolhardy rescue expedition.

But the men at Little America sensed the trouble. Word came that three of them were setting out to come south. Then further word acknowledged that after fifty-two miles they had been forced back. A few days more, and they were on their way again. In due time there came the report that they were ninety-three miles south and sure they would make it. Byrd says that the next hours were almost unbearable in their waiting. As time went on and there was no further word, he fell into the deepest despair. Periodically he climbed the ladder to the surface of the ice to keep the flares burning lest the tractor pass him by in the Antarctic night. When despair reached its depth, he decided to look once more, and climbed the ladder to the surface. He opened the trap door and then, "I blinked my eyes and peered into the north. The fingering beam of a searchlight moved slowly up and down against the black backdrop of the horizon. It might be another hallucination. I sat down, resolutely facing the opposite horizon. When I stood up and looked again, the beam was still fanning up and down. . . . In that miraculous instant all the despair and suffering of June and July dropped away, and I felt as if I had just been born again."[10]

"Just been born again." Familiar words! And what had happened? He was the same man with the same need and in the same situation—with one all-important distinction. A separation was ended. An isolation was broken. He was no longer alone. Born again, indeed!

The meaning of the Christ Event will never be caught to the full in any word or parable, but this is part of it, and for a moment we can use the picture. The Event was the time when "God was in Christ, reconciling the world unto himself." The separation was ended, the alienation overcome.

When we talk of preaching these days, we most likely will insist that the New Testament preaching is proclaiming the *kerugma*, those mighty events of God in the life of Jesus Christ. It is an urgent word, a corrective to the vague and easy moralizing to which some preaching had fallen. But we also need to be sure when we speak of preaching the *kerugma* that we have in mind not only the proclaiming of a past event, but of a present one. It is not only what God in Christ has done, but what He *is* doing, for the Event goes on. It was not once and for all; it was once and for always. We even may borrow some contemporary words to express it. We will not forget the dramatic hour when Churchill said, as the invasion of the Continent began, "This is not the beginning of the end, but only the end of the beginning." In a sense Christian history says that of Christ's earthly ministry. His contemporaries thought it was the beginning of the end, this mighty act of God in Christ. Now we know it was only the end of the beginning. The Event goes on, and whenever the Christian preacher stands to speak the word of Christ and for Christ, God's gracious acts go on. Even now there is "release to the captives and recovering of sight to the blind."

Of course that is an incredible claim! Absolutely audacious! It is either our most awesome truth or our most tragic delusion. Even the preacher backs away from it, as the Psalmist backed away from the knowledge of God, saying, "It is high, I cannot attain unto it." Yet if we seek the Biblical ground of preaching, as we must, this seems to me inescapable, no matter how impossible it may appear. For the Bible *does* relate God's *special* acts of disclosure, the Covenant to the people of Israel, the Kingdom proclaimed by John, and the gospel which pulsates in the Pauline letters. Preaching ought never to settle for a lesser level, simply because the full claim seems impossible. It is always an act of faith and always will be so, transcending reason even though it never suspends it.

Sometimes when we are tempted to feel that this claim runs off the track of reality and falls into fantasy, we may stop to think a moment about an intermediate mystery, the wonder of a word, any word. In a sense it is always a miracle what a word can do, for good or for evil. Born in the heart of one man, it finds its place, when well spoken, in the heart of another. And from that seed come remarkable fruits. A word can enlighten a mind that is darkened, strengthen a will that has grown weak, relive an experience already past, anticipate an experience yet to come. A word can make men hate, or it can awaken love. In short, a word is experience in capsule form, reduced to its essence, imparted to another where it is restored as full experience. Small wonder, then, that words have been used to impart the Word! Where better shall the Event of Christ be kept and imparted than in this wondrous means of bringing the encounter of soul to soul? The Word once become flesh in one

sense has become words again, and entrusted, wonder of wonders, to him who will preach these words in faith. It is as part of
this Event that we find at last our real identity. It is a hope of
vast dimension to believe that preaching thus enables Christ to
do in and for men what he began in his earthly ministry! Those
works go on when preaching is real.

There are, for example, the works of revelation. That was part
of the Event. Men knew what they had not known before, and
all of life was illumined. Recognition became revelation. It was
seeing the significance of that which was at hand or taking place.
The sum of it is in the descriptive words in the Emmaus experience, "And their eyes were opened and they recognized him."
They were the same persons and it was the same situation, but a
reality already present had been recognized.

So the works of disclosure go on where preaching is real.
God has many ways of making Himself known. But when the
great revelation was made, it was not primarily in the natural
or in the supernatural. It was in the human, in One who lived
among us, who "emptied himself, taking the form of a servant."
The universals of human experience become points at which
God confronts us and makes Himself known. That recognition
of God at work in our human situations can take place when
preaching is real.

At other times there are the works of *reconciliation*. The word
is clear, "and gave us the ministry of reconciliation." Christian
preaching is under this amazing commission. When the word is
real and received in faith men make their peace with God,
accept themselves, and come to terms with their brothers. What
a blessed work that is!

Ernie Pyle is known to most of us as a faithful reporter of
the average G.I. during World War II. Pyle himself seemed so
much like the men of whom he wrote, hating war yet knowing
he must be part of it. The greatest struggle Ernie Pyle faced

during the war, however, was not at the front, but in a hotel room in London. Word reached him there of the death of his mother. And alone he struggled with the ultimate questions of the meaning of life, but found no answer. Falling back upon his writing, he recorded his reaction in these poignant words: "It seems to me that life is futile and death the final indignity. People live and suffer and grow bent with yearning, bowed with disappointment, and then they die. And what is it all for? I do not know."[11]

Where shall a man come to terms with such an unanswered question? With such a doubt there must be a great gulf fixed between a man and his God. He must come to terms with such meaninglessness or he is inevitably isolated and alone. Surely the pulpit often must speak to that need, believing that God in Christ is seeking the reconciliation.

Many of us began our preaching in the echo of the term "preaching for a verdict." It is a phrase which seeks to catch the note of urgency and the necessity of decision, certainly essential to real preaching. But increasingly the pastor may find himself turning from the term "verdict" because it has the note of judgment. In reality the judgment is not ours to make. Instead it seems much better to speak of preaching for *consent*. Here we catch more clearly the note of the gospel, the prior will of God, the initiative seeking reconciliation, the knocking at the door of One who has done all and waits for our final word to make the reconciliation complete. On many occasions of preaching there must be the clear overtone of God graciously seeking our consent to be reconciled. An event indeed!

Equally, preaching will be the work of *redemption*. The word is so strong that we often reserve it for the hours of extremity. It should not be so. Just as our bodies are redeemed from destruction by the daily renewal of rest, so a man's whole life needs to be redeemed continuously by God's gifts. To return to

our Father's house before we get very far off the premises is
still a return. Is not a man saved from the far country if he
is brought back at the front gate before all is lost? In a sense the
whole process of life is one of redemption, sometimes in extremity, yet often on the level of our daily need. In our understanding we can see that in preaching, God in Christ is continuously redeeming life.

Again, the preacher must be humbled beyond words at the
thought of such an identity. Yet here we must stand, and here
we must preach, trusting in the divine initiative which makes
possible such an Event.

V. *The Secular Barrier*

When, however, a claim like this appears in our culture, it
must seem alien and not a little fantastic. How do we confirm
such a claim in a secular culture which by its nature has other
foundations than that upon which the claim rests? This in part
is one reason many have lost their identity. To live in a secular
culture like ours, where life is organized apart from God, leaves
the preacher in a groundless calling. For he is trying to ground
his word on precisely the premise which a secular culture omits.

It is not surprising, therefore, that the preacher's claim is really
not taken seriously by many contemporaries. It is not met
by open opposition as much as quiet indifference. It is not in
acts of renunciation, but in assumptions of irrelevance. Just as
in flight there is a crucial point called the sound barrier, so in
the penetration of our culture with the gospel there seems a
point we can call the secular barrier. Here life, organized apart
from God, comes to its maximum resistance to a word of God
which, once accepted, would force its complete reordering. To
such a barrier we often come when the preacher really speaks to
the modern world. We sense that barrier at several points.

One of them is in the minister himself. We too are sons of our time. The ambivalence is in us. We have our hours of being completely overwhelmed by the height of the claim upon which our preaching must rest, and must find some way of handling the tension. The fact is that a preacher usually does not feel the way he thinks he ought to feel if he really were what he claims to be.

There are hours when we would have great sympathy with the words which Stephen Vincent Benét attributes to Abraham Lincoln. We have known this query:

> What is God's will?
> They come to me and talk about God's will
> In righteous deputations and platoons,
> Day after day, laymen and ministers.
> They write me Prayers From Twenty Million Souls
> Defining me God's will and Horace Greeley's.
> God's will is General This and Senator That,
> God's will is those poor colored fellows' will,
> It is the will of the Chicago churches,
> It is this man's and his worst enemy's.
>
> But all of them are sure they know God's will
> I am the only man who does not know it.
> And, yet, if it is probable that God
> Should, and so very clearly, state His will
> To others, on a point of my own duty,
> It might be thought He would reveal it me
> Directly, more especially as I
> So earnestly desire to know His will.[12]

Who has not known such hours? If God really has willed to make Himself known, why is it so difficult to know Him? There is no easy answer to that. We know only that preaching, like prayer, is labor and sometimes anguish. Before the initiative of God, at once imperious and patient, we struggle to contain a word that can be understood and communicated. The secular mind in the preacher himself trims his words and brings times of great hesitation. He will know hours when he wonders whether the challenge ever can be overcome.

Moreover, our preached words often seem more secular than God-given. Even Emil Brunner, whose belief in revelation is beyond dispute, is forced to confess: "What a torrent of nonsense, superstitions, delusions, and emotional fantasies have been poured out at all times into the life of humanity under the cover of the claim of revelation."[13]

We must have great sympathy with those who listen for the authentic word in preaching but fail to hear it, sensing only the contradictions, inconsistencies, and clear overtones of our own self-interest. Recently I chose to preach on the subject "It's Not As Late As You Think." Quite by chance another pastor selected for that day the subject "It Is Later than You Think." So the two subjects were listed side by side in the church columns the night before! We can't even agree what time it is!

In far more serious ways, many a person open and eager to hear an authentic word to illumine the contradictions of his life has to turn away, concluding wistfully that we have no word more enlightened than that which comes from men who claim no special revelation. The word they hear carries for them no credential or authority. It seems to them to reflect all the contradictions, special pleading, and self-interest which makes up the pronouncements of men in other fields. Surely if it is of God, men feel, it should be different. Yet is it? The resistance at the secular barrier believes it is not. The voice they hear sounds strangely like their own.

Yet even deeper there is a resistance because much secularism does not understand the need to which the gospel is addressed. It is at this point that we must restore the distinction to the word "news" as Christians use it. The repeated handling of the word in our common life has made it mean something quite different from the sense in which the gospel is "good news." News, as we hear it daily, most often is information, usually information about other people. It confronts us with no decision; it leaves us with no need of response; it implants no radical hope. Yet in the gospel sense "the news" is vastly different. It is proclaimed to those who are *involved*. It is not information; it is tidings for which we have been waiting, changing the whole situation of our lives.

Let us put it into a picture actually taken from the news. One morning the news brought word that a plane was down between Hawaii and Johnston Island. It informed us that search planes were out looking for survivors. The evening news brought word that a raft had been sighted and rescue was on the way. We all heard this with interest and a moment of thankfulness that lost men had been found.

But how different our response must have been compared to that of the men on the raft! To us it was a casual if interesting word; to them it was a word of life. They had been sighted, and the outcome was assured. Now the "news," as we proclaim it in the gospel, is like that which came to the men on the raft. It is not information about someone else; it is a tidings brought to those involved.

So we sense the meaning of the news by thinking of it as related in kind to some common human experiences. When we have waited through the night with a loved one in crisis and learned that the outcome is to be life; when we have walked on the abyss of anxiety and first felt the strengthening hand of assurance; when we have known the awful loneliness of separation and heard the footstep of someone returning whom we love, then, in such times, we begin to sense the meaning of the word "news" as the gospel proclaims it.

But how shall the word come with full impact to men who are not aware of their condition to which the word speaks? How shall we offer the word of life to those who do not know that life without God is under judgment? Here indeed is one part of the Event of Christ in preaching. It is first illumination of the real human situation that men, seeing life as it is, may hear the word as it is. No commission is more urgent upon the contemporary preacher than this. Like John, he must prepare the way for Christ's coming to modern men.

VI. *The Preacher's Real Engagement*

See where our inquiry then has brought us. To know what we are as preachers has become a compelling necessity. Rightly handled, it is a question that can lead us to new depth of preaching. But the answer will not be found in the institutional or the psychological, in the liturgical or the cultural, or in the subjective relationship alone. The central ground of our ministry is theological, and our preaching is an act of faith in God's disclosure of Himself in many and diverse ways, coming to consummation in the great Event of Jesus Christ.

Yet the assumption upon which we preach is precisely the omission of a secular society. Here is our uncertainty. Here is the tension under which the modern preacher must live. As Reinhold Niebuhr has pointed out, we who preach in America find ourselves in a day that is strangely religious and secular at the same time. "We are 'religious,'" says Dr. Niebuhr, "in the sense that religious communities enjoy the devotion and engage the active loyalty of more laymen than in any nation of the Western world. We are 'secular' in the sense that we pursue the immediate goals of life, without asking too many ultimate questions about the meaning of life and without being too disturbed by the tragedies and antinomies of life."[14]

Because this is true the preacher's real engagement is to enter vigorously into the conversation in which the secular way of life is challenged, occasionally supported, and often judged, but always in the light of another way that is open. The pulpit stands precisely at this point in our time where these two ways of life engage in struggle and bid for the souls of men.

Hence the preacher must understand both the marks of his time and the marks of the gospel. For he cannot carry out his main engagement without this dual understanding. Again and again he will know his insufficiency, yet he preaches in faith, believing in Him "who by the power at work within us is able to do far more abundantly than all we ask or think." So there is an answer to the question with which the devoted preacher must grapple all his life. It is proclaimed in the great hymn:

> How firm a foundation, ye saints of the Lord,
> Is laid for your faith in His excellent word!
> What more can He say than to you He hath said?

What more indeed! And what else can we do but stand up and preach it humbly and joyously!

CHAPTER TWO

The Sermon:

SOMETHING OUT OF THE ORDINARY

IN THE FAST-MOVING NARRATIVE OF SAMUEL there is a single verse which on occasion must try the soul of any preacher. The same chapter which tells of Samuel's classic call closes with this summary, "And Samuel grew, and the Lord was with him and let none of his words fall to the ground." None of them; that is quite an average! In the face of it, we who are lesser men painfully recall those hours when we have covered the ground with our words. Who could read of Samuel without envy?

Yet it happens. In spite of our best efforts our words often fall to the ground. It is a long fall from the high theological claim of preaching to the level of the average sermon.

So we must come to terms with the actual hour of preaching. What a familiar scene! The people gather at the appointed time, according to their custom. Though, in theory, they reserve this hour for eternal affairs, actually they bring the world with them in a diversity of gifts and needs. Some are weary and some are angry. Some have come because it is their habit. Others know a strange compulsion. There are the seeking, the complacent, the hungry, the anxious, the discouraged. There are also those who come that particular day with a sense that they are keeping an appointment of soul; a strange readiness is about them, the whole issue of life seems to hang in so close a balance that a persuasive word can make the difference.

The service proceeds along a traditional way, for some a rich and ancient liturgy, for others a simple ordering of the elements of divine worship, for some a kind of comfortable disorder, a formalized informality. For all there will be music, prayers, and the reading of ancient, cherished words. Then for most the moment comes, that tremendous moment, when a man must stand up to preach. As his words begin, they often seem, especially to the casual onlooker, very ordinary and earthbound. There are no opening skies. There is no angel visitant. Often it seems but another vain repetition. In short, by every external evidence, it is a very ordinary occasion.

The recalling of such a time brings a haunting question: Is the Word, the very Word of God, to be heard in so prosaic an occasion? Can the event of Christ really be in such an everyday happening? Of all the ways in which a majestic God might disclose Himself, does this not seem the least promising? Can so much really hinge on so little?

Yet faith repeatedly comes back with an answer that common sense cannot know. It begins with confession that often, all too often, it *is* vain repetition. Affirmation that God's Word is in such an occasion often may grow faint, but it never dies out. Something in us rises to respond to an assurance like that of Brunner:

"Where there is true preaching, where, in the obedience of faith, the Word is proclaimed, there, in spite of all appearances to the contrary, the most important thing that ever happens upon this earth takes place."[1]

What then are the deeper elements which converge to transform this ordinary hour into the great Event? It is not given us to create the possibility: that is God's part. But by diligent preparation we can increase the probability of the moment; that is our part. As a people of God we can make faithful preparation for the hour of preaching which will offer Christ every hospitality and, as it were, fling open the door to a well-prepared house when we invite him to come. Even these preparations cannot guarantee that God's gracious Word will be in our words when they are preached. When we have done all, there will be times of strange silence and seeming withdrawal for which there is no real explanation. But there is evidence enough, and more, that, ordinary though the occasion may seem, the work of Christ goes on where the Word of him is preached. To be sure, it is God's gift, but it is not bestowed on those who come casually, failing to understand that the receiving itself is a momentous responsibility. To honor that possibility is one purpose of preaching.

As we search for those elements which make the preaching situation distinctive in the experience of men, we often must describe where we cannot define. Like other sources of power, the power of preaching will be accepted at times even when it cannot be understood. Yet there are conditions about that hour of preaching which disclose themselves with marked constancy. They are always met when preaching is real. We shall consider the essential elements as follows: our belief, our remembrance, the pew, the word, and Christian love. Within the commonplace gathering of a Sunday morning these elements are present, fused into one great experience of the disclosure of God.

I. Belief: The Great Expectancy

The first element in the preaching situation is an intangible quality, yet discernibly real. It is specific *belief*. This does not mean, of course, the holding of a given body of doctrine or only the intellectual assent to a set of propositions. The belief that opens the door to the creative experience of preaching is a confidence that God's promise to disclose Himself is greatly to be trusted, and that the Event of Christ *is* still going on, as proclaimed. Paul wrote to the Corinthians, "We too believe, and so we speak." For Paul that was clearly a confidence in the living Christ. That belief brings an assured expectancy which enfolds both pastor and people. The evidences of that belief are discernible in the hours of worship: an openness, a deep seriousness, a confession of need, a readiness for obedience, and a consciousness of being a committed community waiting upon God. This fusion of assurance and expectancy, penetrating the whole preaching situation, seems to be the quality which, in turn, receives the Event. Perhaps, after all, it is best summed up in the Biblical phrase, "waiting upon God." Here are all the elements of that expectancy: the assurance, the awesome awareness of another, the willingness to hear as well as to speak, the openness to the things that are unseen but eternal.

How difficult it is to put such a reality into words. Yet how impossible to bring Christian preaching to its fulfillment without it! The claim of preaching rests at last upon the affirmation which well may be called the essence of Christian fellowship, "Where two or three are gathered in my name, *there am I.*" Christian koinonia is not merely then a high form of "togetherness," though many churches seem to make it so. But this is a gathering infused with a special assurance and expectancy. The two or three, or many more, come secondarily to face one another, but primarily to be confronted by another who has said, "There am I." This lifts the Christian experience forever above the vague, the esoteric, and the hidden. It gives a definite locus to the great disclosure. It is the ground in which preaching is redeemed from the ordinary words of men to the saving Word of God. It is the power of a great expectation.

II. Remembrance: Recalling What God Has Done

Once again, preaching can be understood only in the total dialogue of worship. In our time we have recovered, even in churches traditionally informal, the importance of the integrity of the service where the sermon is preached. It is commonly said that in the Bible there are three directions in which the words are addressed. Some are from man to God; others are from man to man about God; and others are from God to men. Even so, in any full service of worship dialogue must go on in all three directions. Some of the acts of worship are points at which we address our words to God. The sermon becomes in turn the point at which God's Word is addressed to us.

One essential part of worship is the deliberate recalling of God's wondrous acts toward men. To recall all He has done is to recover the assurance of what He is doing. Perhaps this is the reason we are so often counseled in the Bible to *remember*, deliberately to "forget not all His benefits." So, properly in any full service the sermon will be closely related to this element of worship in which we have renewed our belief by remembering and giving thanks for all God has done.

This aspect of remembrance and recognition is seen in several ways. It is the distinctive mark of the service of Communion, which begins in remembrance but ends looking forward in hope. "Do this in remembrance of me," we hear as we take the bread. "You proclaim the Lord's death until he comes," we are told as we take the cup. Thus we remember, and thus we recover our hope. The service is not complete without both.

It is the same note which is caught in the words of John Henry Newman. "So long Thy power hath blest me," he confesses. But his next words are hope and expectation, born from the remembering. "Sure it still will lead me on, o'er moor and fen, o'er crag and torrent, till the night is gone." John Baillie has confessed that in a similar act of devotion he was brought back to fellowship in the hours when God seemed remote. When all was dark, he began to recall God's gracious gifts. It was as though the stars came out one by one until the whole firmament of his faith was alive again. This *is* worship, having remembrance leading to recognition, and recognition leading to expectancy.

This is one of the important ways in which preaching must be Biblical. Our faith *is* historically grounded. We possess it by going again and again to those special acts of God which are related and interpreted in the Biblical record. Our faith in God's immediacy rests upon the recalling of these disclosures of God's sufficiency. It reflects the confidence that God *is* acting because we know that He has acted in the past. So we come to the moments of preaching with our faith lifted to a higher level because we have remembered and worshiped God.

Real worship often may be pictured by a scene I knew as a boy in the Ohio Valley. The river was navigable only because a series of locks had been built to help boats accommodate to the changing levels of the river. Such a lock rests upon a simple engineering concept. A boat enters on the lower level and a gate closes behind. Then the water pours into the lock, lifting the boat to the higher level. Then another gate opens and the craft moves out on the new level which has been achieved. In a similar way, true worship brings us to the time of preaching with our faith already lifted to higher levels. By remembering and giving thanks we have restored our confidence that God who has spoken is speaking, and so we came to listen.

III. The Pew: An Exposed Position

We turn now to consider an important element of the preaching situation, namely, the pew. Obviously it is essential!

Yet often we do not do justice to the active part the pew plays in the preaching experience. In this, too, we lose the meaning because it seems so commonplace.

Yet weigh this matter for a moment. Is it not true that the pew represents one of the few exposed positions in our contemporary culture? When preaching becomes real, here, as at few points, the listener lays open the center of his life for re-examination and exposure. Here in the seeming privacy and anonymity of the pew, a person weighs the great questions of his life, the values he is seeking, the moral decisions he is facing or evading, the basic reliances by which he is living, the direction and destiny of the years. In short, the pew is one place where the ultimate and the intimate meet. The word one hears is about deep things, affecting the whole person. Here one is led to consider matters he faces nowhere else: sin and forgiveness, prayer and one's relation to God, the basic ethical standards by which life must be guided. This means that moments in the pew can be counted among those intimate times, often lost in our culture, when life is uncovered and the center is exposed. It is closest to the quiet moments that come between those who love each other, or the moments of encounter with a trusted counselor. There is, indeed, something real which may be called the public privacy of the pew.

The recognition of this truth requires us who preach to take some further important factors into account. In my judgment, we have not fully recognized this active part of the pew in the whole experience of preaching. If preaching is a real person-to-person engagement, then the listener is far from passive, but indeed has his own active part to play. It brings us to recognize some essential truths.

One of those is to understand that preaching is always a one-to-one relationship. By first appearance it seems to be a one-to-many situation. To be sure, there is a difference in the way in which one listens as a member of a congregation. Yet preaching by its nature essentially is always to one person. More exactly, it is many one-to-one relationships taking place simultaneously. The *preached* word is also the *heard* word—and each hears with his own experience. The preacher will need to take into account the simple fact he is engaged not in monologue but in a conversation. At points in his preaching his sermon will need to reflect the reaction of those to whom he is preaching. This is an important part of the sensitivity of the preacher. He must show that he knows the hearer as well as the word. Not only must he be aware of God's disclosure, but he must also be sensitive to the acceptances and resistances which are in the listener. So the worshiper must feel that in the preacher he too has a voice. He is an active part of the conversation, a subject acting, not an object acted upon.

Some years ago when I was traveling in the Orient, it was difficult for mail to catch up with me. This meant that while those at home were hearing from me regularly, my letters rarely reflected any word I had received from them. My wife tells me that this was a very frustrating experience. I never answered a question which she had asked, nor showed any awareness of experiences at home which she had reported. So we were in contact, but we were not in conversation. There was no real interchange, no reflection of the other's experience in the letters we wrote. Sometimes the worshiper must have a similar feeling about the sermon. It never reflects his reaction, and gives no evidence of taking into account the questions he must be raising, or of confirming agreements he is affirming. This also is contact without conversation. A respect for the integrity of the pew will bring that quality of reflection—reflection of the persons who hear—into the preaching of the Word.

Considering further the significance of the pew, we need to emphasize the importance of expectant belief in the worshiper.

Not only in the preaching of the Word, but in the receiving of it, the awareness of the Event of Christ is an essential element. The writer of Hebrews noted this when he wrote in another relation, "The message which they heard did not benefit them, because it did not meet with faith in the hearers."[2] Thus it is not only deep that speaks to deep, but faith that speaks to faith. This is a part of "the partnership in the gospel," as Paul expressed it to the Philippians, in which the preacher and the worshiper know that they are under God and together waiting for the Event.

In this relation the pastor has an obligation, it seems to me, to lead the congregation into the fuller meaning of the preaching experience. If, as we are saying, the Word preached is sacrament, then it follows that there must be a necessary preparation for receiving it. With great care we try to prepare those who are to receive sacraments of the church in other ways. We would consider ourselves remiss in the pastoral responsibility if we allowed anyone to receive a sacrament without the proper preparation of heart and mind. Yet in most of our pastorates we preach year after year without ever imparting to those who worship, the nature of the act in which we are engaged. Does it not follow that one of the most urgent needs in pastoral preaching is the training of the congregation for its part in it? It seems to me appropriate and even urgent that on occasion there should be a sermon about the faith upon which preaching rests. Certainly in those smaller groups where the minister is engaged in training people for the Christian life, he should include some interpretation of the meaning of preaching in our Protestant tradition and the ways in which the sacrament of the Word is received. To Paul's word, "We believe and therefore we speak," well may be added the affirmation of the listener, "We also believe and therefore we receive."

Another aspect of this is a recognition that beside the freedom of the pulpit, there is the corresponding freedom of the pew. This too is a right won at tremendous cost. The Protestant tradition therefore rests upon two freedoms, not one. There is the freedom of the pulpit in which the congregation cannot tell the preacher what he must preach, or what he may not. But there is also the freedom of the pew in which the minister may neither require the assent nor prohibit the dissent of the worshiper. Between these two freedoms, we believe there is ample room for the gift of God's Word to come with freshness and power.

In our time both these freedoms are endangered. But the danger is not so much tyranny, which has cast its shadow in the past, as anarchy in which the freedoms are misused or abused irresponsibly. We are prone to conclude that we have used our respective freedoms responsibly when, on the one hand, the minister has spoken, and on the other hand, the worshiper has sat through it! Yet both freedoms must be under authority, the authority of Christ as Lord of the Church. Full freedom is always maintained only when it is also aware of the authority under which it lives. We have not fulfilled freedom responsibly when we have only spoken and heard. There must be a speaking that *expects* to be heard and a hearing which *intends* to receive. In short, it is the freedom of a committed community. It is the freedom of those who are under orders and know the meaning of Paul's phrase, "The love of Christ controls us." In this sense the significance of the freedom of the pew in the act of preaching must also be recovered if the claim is to be fulfilled.

There is one further consideration of the place of the pew. What is it that listeners may hope to receive? Is it a new idea, or a deeper resolve, or, on occasion, a clarification of some great historic doctrine? These are part of it. But while they have their place in a full program of preaching, none alone is the great gift.

The deeper reality is that preaching actually brings new qualities of life to those who share in the experience. It is not an idea about the Christian life; it is life itself which is given. In a profound way the real experience is one of personal fulfillment and re-creation. When preaching is at its highest a man comes away from it saying not simply "I ought," though there are great ethical imperatives, nor "I will," though there are great decisions. Deeper than these, he comes away saying "I am"; for to some degree, or in some aspect, he is a new creation. Something has happened in him and to him. The mark of the preaching is not something he has heard, but something he has become. It is not a new definition he has received, but a new dimension of life itself.

With notable consensus sensitive souls have spoken of this many times. In a sense they have affirmed what J. N. Grou said in another respect, "Christ does not teach humility but bestows it."[3] That is it exactly! When preaching is real, God *bestows* new gifts of life. Thomas à Kempis touched the same truth in another way: "I would rather feel compunction than be able to define it."[4] One would rather receive it than hear a point-by-point description of it. That receiving is the great promise of preaching at its highest. It does not simply talk about hope or courage or strength or newness of life; it bestows them. It is an audacious thing to claim, but there is no escape from it. By God's grace the sermon becomes a clear channel for the gifts that fulfill life. In the preached word the divine processes of personal fulfillment and redemption go on. It is in this sense that we can say that when preaching is real God is acting. The word He brings is not only something about Himself; it is a word that says something about us, too. As in the Bible, the word often is one of creation and release; God is saying, "Let there be light," or "Let there be life," or "Let there be love."

Small wonder that we turn from this as something too great to expect from so ordinary an occasion. Is it not really making it all too simple? When we set this claim down beside the long and painful process by which old habits ordinarily are replaced by new, we may wonder if the claim of wholeness and fulfillment through preaching is not too naïve for our sophisticated culture, too close to magic for comfort. Yet the whole meaning of this belief must be seen. This does not say that God's wondrous work in any life breaks in at a single moment of preaching alone. For the listener every sermon has its antecedents and its consequences. It is an awesome truth that God has been so preparing a life that the encounter of a sermon may be the determining influence in the great issues, the last ounce that tips the scale.

Boswell once said of his friendship for Dr. Johnson that it came about as drops of water falling one by one into a cup, causing it at last to overflow. But which drop made it overflow? It could not have happened without all of them. It is not given to the preacher to know how many drops have fallen into the cup of the worshiper's experience before the hour of preaching.

There is ample testimony that this is precisely the way God's work has been done in many lives. William Wilberforce wrote about the influence of Isaac Milner upon his life. There was no one moment which seemed decisive. Milner, a distinguished schoolmaster at Hull, traveled on the Continent with Wilberforce for two summers. Milner had been deeply affected by the evangelical movement of the eighteenth century. In their conversation and their reading he led Wilberforce to think along new lines. In the second summer they read the Greek New Testament together. By this repeated encounter there came to Wilberforce the truth which changed his life. "By gradual degrees," he said later, "I imbibed his sentiments though I must confess with shame that they long remained merely as opinions assented to by my understanding but not influencing my heart." More than Wilberforce knew, however, the impact had been made. He moved into months of soul-searching, and after further counsel with John Newton, then dean of St. Paul's, he emerged onto a new level of life which he called "a serenity, tranquility, composure which is not to be destroyed."[5] Through long years of social struggle in England, especially for the freedom of the slaves, that composure remained.

This is a revealing description, it would seem, of the influence upon a life which week after week hears the Word of Christ preached. Many of us could never point to a single hour when the cup overflowed into newness of life. But we would still acknowledge that the repeated encounter in the hour of preaching has brought an accumulated fullness without which our lives would have been radically different. It is this truth which sustains the minister who preaches in the pastorate Sunday after Sunday and sometimes wonders whether anything is happening. Where the Word is really preached and received faithfully, there is a continued and cumulative gift of life. It is this assurance which can bring the worshiper to his pew with expectation, and the preacher to his study with hope!

The sum of it is that both pulpit and pew must be engaged in the partnership of the gospel. If, as we are saying often these days, preaching must be understood as encounter, it follows that we must prepare those in the pew who are to share the encounter. If, as we also say, the church means the people of God, then preaching must involve all the people. If the Word, as we further affirm, is sacrament, then how can it be received without proper preparation? In short, every recovery in the claim of preaching today brings us with new urgency to consider the part of the worshiper in the pew as well as the preacher in his pulpit in bringing the claim to fulfillment.

IV. *The Word: Elements of an Art*

This brings us to the sermon itself. It is the only instrument we have for achieving these ends. Sometimes the use of the sermon has been called a science. But more exactly, it seems to me an art, because it is the communication of experience. John Ciardi once noted in the *Saturday Review* that "writing means the art of shaping experience into a form that releases the experience to the reader."[6] In a similar sense preaching must be understood as the art which shapes experience into the form of a sermon which in turn releases the experience to those who hear. What a demanding art that is!

To communicate any experience is a miracle. But when it is the experience of God, who is sufficient for such a responsibility? When the experience to be imparted is the encounter with God that brings new meaning to life, then surely it becomes the highest of the arts. And the sermon must be made as fitting an instrument as we can fashion. Nothing is more deadly than our becoming mere mechanics or technicians in preaching. But neither can we let failures of craftsmanship stand in the way of the freshness and renewal which are gifts of the Spirit. In all honesty, we must confess that again and again it is our crudities and undisciplined preparation which stand in the way of real communication in preaching. To be insufficient is one thing; to be careless is quite another. So when we seek a mastery of specific skills it is that the sermon may become an adequate instrument worthy of our claim. Several elements require our consideration.

1. *Interest.* Here is one part of preaching which should be discussed but on which there seems to be a conspiracy of silence. It is the basic quality of interest. The fact is, our words, unlike Samuel's, often fall to the ground simply because they are so dull and uninteresting. How does it happen that so often we take the word of life and make it lifeless? If the gospel is good

news, then obviously it ought to be vibrant and pulsating instead of deadly and dull. What makes for interest? Can we put our finger upon the quality?

We must see the contrast, at the outset, between simply attracting attention and gaining interest. Attracting attention may make a man an onlooker, but it does not make him a participant. Real interest comes when one feels himself involved, or to use a better word, "addressed," as Martin Buber would put it. This, I think, more than any device or any homiletic skill, is the secret of real interest. We are interested in that which involves us. Let it become clear that a sermon is dealing with the living options which confront a person, and inevitably he becomes interested in the outcome. Disengaged preaching which does not address a person in the living situation inevitably becomes dull because it is irrelevant, dealing with no living options.

Some years ago after a busy winter season our family took a brief holiday in Death Valley. In a museum near our inn were mementoes and reminders of the days when parties sought to cross the desert to reach California. My interest was drawn particularly to a diary which recorded the experience of one of these parties. The diarist relates that included in the group was a New England minister who was crossing the continent with his family. On the very day when the party crossing Death Valley came to dire distress, it is written that the minister was seen gathering his family in the shadow of one of the wagons to deliver a lecture on the values of higher education! While he was thus engaged in this irrelevance, other men in the party made the real decisions. Two of them set out by foot, crossed the remainder of the desert, went over the Panamint Mountains into California. Almost without resting they started back with horses and supplies and reached the waiting party in time to save them from death.

Sometimes I wonder whether my ministerial brother ever had at least a twinge of conscience about his utter irrelevance when the real decisions were being made. While he was delivering a sermon, other men were delivering people. We may be sure that preaching is meant to be the latter. But that does mean dealing with the living options.

This seems to me to open an insight about preaching as an art. It is of course true that preaching, if it is to be interesting, must be dramatic. This means in part that in the sermon, as in a drama, there must be a sense of identification felt by those who hear. Yet here there emerges an important distinction. It appears that the identification of the listener to the sermon is almost the opposite of that of the spectator of a drama. When a drama is effective there is an unmistakable identification of those who view it. As the story unfolds the spectator finds himself, as it were, drawn onto the stage to share in the action taking place before him. Unconsciously, if the drama is effective, he increasingly feels with its characters "I am that." By a kind of empathy he is lifted into the drama to play another's role for a little while. He is, as we say, lifted out of himself. This can be a profound experience, as everyone who has shared great drama can testify.

But consider in contrast the identification in preaching. When it is real the worshiper is not lifted out of himself but rather, like the Prodigal, comes to himself. In a sense the identification moves in the reverse direction. Something moves out of the preached word to identify itself with the listener. Thus he is not called to play a role for the time being. He is led to set aside the false roles he has been playing and at last to become himself. He says as the gospel is preached, "That is I." Drama can be an escape from reality, but preaching is the discovery of it and the return to it. The excitement of dynamic preaching is the awareness that this kind of identification is taking place.

It enables one to speak of the preacher in the oft-quoted comment about John Wesley, "He understands all the secrets of my heart." When that kind of identification—the gospel with the person and the person with the gospel—is taking place, there will be interest, profound, absorbing, inescapable.

2. *Structure.* Equally, there rests upon the preacher the obligation to find the form by which a given truth can be communicated. We have rebelled, and rightly, against the over-emphasis upon a traditional form. It is tiresome indeed, and ultimately ineffective, to assume that truth always comes with three points and a poem. But this does not lessen the importance of appropriate structure in the essential business of communicating a truth. Phillips Brooks well said, "There is nothing a sermon ought to be except a medium of truth to men." True, but it also follows that only with sound structure can a sermon be an adequate medium.

We have never been released from the basic requirements of unity, coherence, and emphasis in the establishment of structure for the sermon. Among ourselves we can wonder at the number of times when we have heard a preacher dealing with the truth which was important and urgent, but which failed to reach its hearers because it was not put in a form which took into account basic laws of listening.

In our theological resurgence we have come to speak of preaching again as proclamation. It is indeed recalling God's wondrous acts; it is proclaiming actual realities, not merely arousing vague feelings. But proclamation alone is not enough. The gospel needs a preacher simply because someone must put it in a form which can be communicated. How shall we state the gospel to make it understood in our culture? The recovery of the gospel is important, but so is its communication.

The judgment about proper structure is no small part of the minister's preparation for preaching. It is a widely held principle that "function determines form." We see this in architecture or technology or even in art. So the nature of the truth preached in a sermon helps to determine its forms. This *is* the task of the preacher as against the theologian. It is he who must be the bridge between the saving truth and the person to be saved. He has not fulfilled his own calling until he has learned the skills and made the judgments which will find the proper structure for the truth he preaches. Sometimes it will be a structure which faces contemporary challenges and gives the Christian alternatives; sometimes it will be deductive, stating a truth and enlarging upon its implications; sometimes it will be inductive, starting with evidence at hand and leading on to the more inclusive truth which the gospel brings. But always in the mind of the preacher there must be some clear sense of structure.

3. *Emotion.* Still further in the art of preaching there is a recognition of the inevitable place of emotion in communication. Having seen emotion used for its own sake and made cheap we often try to keep it out of the sermon. Especially we who recognize the importance of the intellectual ground of the gospel look with great reservations upon preaching which shows much emotion.

Yet really to hear the gospel must be by its nature a moving experience. Simply because emotion can become false, contrived, and artificial does not mean that we can deny that deep feeling is a part of great preaching. When it is used for its own sake, emotion becomes cheap and unhealthy. But when it comes as a sincere response to the meaning of the gospel, it is cleansing and lifting and a power for good.

In earlier years of my ministry I was pastor near a college campus on which Miss Maude Adams, the distinguished American actress, was a teacher. She was a deeply religious person, and we often talked about the relation of religion to the art she represented. She said that in teaching drama she had to say to those in her class, "In other classes you are asked, 'What do you think about this?' But here you will be asked, 'How do you feel about this?' Then you must learn to make others feel about it as you do. This is the meaning of drama."

So the preacher cannot escape revealing how he feels about the truth he proclaims as well as what he thinks about it. Henry Drummond once said, "Christianity does not need more advocates, it needs more witnesses." In this is a real insight. It means that the preacher must be speaking of something in which he is profoundly involved emotionally.

In fact, the release of emotion often is the delicate point at which a sermon moves either to greatness or to cheapness. By this mark the masters of the preaching art have been known. Emotion was a natural, yet controlled, part of their preaching. One of the biographers of George Meredith summarizes his strength as a writer in revealing words. J. B. Priestley says of him that he "is an extremely faulty story teller, and yet contrives to enlarge the whole scope of the art . . . his style is such that it cannot always cope with the expository and other matter that forms the ground level of fiction . . . and yet it shows itself capable of handling the heightened moments, the great scenes in a fashion that lifts such passages far beyond the reach of any but the great masters of the novel."[7]

We have heard preaching like that. It somehow had the capacity for handling the great moments, and often they were revelations of deep feeling of concern or joy. There is an unmistakable mastery of the great emotions which must come only by the most faithful discipline and the deepest grounding in the faith we proclaim. It is true that deep calls unto deep when a man in speaking of a truth adds to intellectual integrity, emotional profundity.

4. *Language.* But where are the words to be found which can

convey the Word? Even as we consider it we realize that any one element of the sermon whether it is structure or emotion or the capturing of interest can become an end in itself rather than a means. At that point the sermon ceases to be the conveying of a truth and becomes an end in itself. Especially is this true of the language of preaching. One must have a profound respect for the words he uses. Yet paradoxically he must never come to value words for their own sake. We preachers are in danger of being described by Stephen Vincent Benét, who in his *Western Star* causes the frontier singer to say:

> We pick our words like nuggets for the shine
> And when they don't fit, we make them fit.[8]

As members of a believing community we have been given some words which belong especially to us. They are words which were born out of travail and have been deepened by centuries of experience. In a sense, the words we use mean more now than when they first were written. They take on meaning by the accumulated experience of those who have lived by them. Perhaps this is seen most vividly in the words we use about the meaning of Jesus Christ. The New Testament inevitably uses words which were current in New Testament times. So the writers spoke of Christ as sacrifice, ransom, high priest, or Logos.

Yet we must face the reality that these are the words of a believing community. They are household words in the family of faith. A part of our function as preachers is to find the words in our culture which will convey the essential truth to those who are outside looking in. Those to whom we preach have never lived under a system of religious sacrifice or in a culture where a man was set free by ransom. Most of us have never known a high priest or used the categories of thought familiar to the Greek. As preachers, our special calling, in part, is to find the words which will help those in our generation understand the gospel, first stated in terms of a distant generation. In a sense the preacher is not unlike the translator who must take the original language and restate the truth in a way which will be understood by the people.

How often we will search for the words to say it! It is significant that Jesus most often cast his truth in the language of relationships—God as Father and other men as brothers. Again and again we use these words of Jesus because the language of relationships is timeless, concrete, relevant, and related to everyday experience. So to our concern and our urgency we must add the skill with words which will make the gospel available to those who first need to understand. It is a mark of our mastery as preachers. Pascal was once accused of using Montaigne's ideas. To which he replied, "Do you say I use the same words as another? Two tennis players use the same ball, but one of them places it better."[9] That too is the skill of preaching!

5. *Illustration*. But now we must consider illustration and its place in the sermon. Need we say that it is far more important to have something to illustrate? Like a light, it is not meant so much to call attention to itself, as illuminate something else.

Yet the pitfalls are many. One of them is illustrated in a rather humorous reference to Wordsworth which is included in *Kilvert's Diary*. Kilvert was an Anglican clergyman who ministered in a small parish in South England a hundred years ago. After his death the remarkably complete diary was discovered in which he recorded the everyday happenings of a parish minister. On September 28, 1870, he tells of a meeting one evening with Wordsworth who came sauntering down the road "crooning aloud some lines of a poem he was composing." When Kilvert stopped his horse and apologized for having intruded, Wordsworth replied, "I am glad I met you for I want to consult you about some lines I am composing in which I want to make the shadow of Etna fall across Syracuse, the mountain being forty miles from the city. Would this be possible?" Kilvert replied that there was nothing in the distance to prevent the shadow of the mountain falling across the city. The only difficulty was that Etna was on the wrong side of the city, being exactly north. To which Wordsworth replied, "Surely it is a little northeast or northwest?" Kilvert added, "As he was determined to make the shadow fall the way he wanted it, I did not contradict him."[10]

Some of our illustrations have fared no better in our hands! Yet the illustration which has integrity and simplicity does give a picture by which a truth can be understood. It further helps often to impart the emotional tone which that truth calls out. Moreover, it offers a chance for the mind to catch up with the unfolding thought processes of the sermon, providing a helpful cadence in the development of a theme.

One important point is to recognize that any illustration needs to be related only to that portion of the sermon to which the thought has come. We must not assume that every illustration must throw light on the whole sermon. It need forward only the thought at the point at which it is used. There will be some occasions when the whole sermon may be seen in the context of a single illustration. But most often it will be only a single stage of development.

Even to mention the elements of a sermon in so cursory a fashion is to recognize that in preaching, as in any art, the secret seems to be a balance, a blending of all of these into one totality called the sermon. Too much concern for structure, or the use of emotion for its own sake, or an undue fondness for language, or an excessive use of illustration can distort and ultimately destroy the art that is in preaching. But when all are seen as instruments to one end, the disclosure and communication of a living truth, then they become the tools by which we fulfill our calling. Preaching is an art by which we find the form that releases the experience to those who hear.

The Sermon

V. Love: The Greatest of These

Yet we must sense that there is one more essential aspect of the preaching situation. Without it we do not invite the Event. This is the prime importance of a real pastoral concern and compassion in the preacher. It is regrettable that the 13th chapter of I Corinthians ever was separated from the 12th. In the 13th Paul was still talking about the gifts to be used within the church, and the greatest of these was agape, that special quality of love which has been called out in us by the gift of Christ— a gift from One who first loved us. And that quality of life is never more real than in the pulpit. Above all else which is communicated, there must be the genuine love of the preacher for the people, and it must be for all of them, not only for those who love him and for those whom he finds lovable, but for all, the unloving and the unlovable! Without this reality our words surely fall to the ground.

There is an appealing picture of John Chrysostom which reflects this pastoral gift. We read that in the second sermon he preached at Antioch he began by saying, "I have addressed you only on one day, and from that day I have loved you as much as though I had been brought up among you."[11] It is precisely this quality which confirms that in the long run the best Christian preaching is pastoral in its concern. It means that the word of the preacher on Sunday will be supported by the faithfulness of his care and compassion during the week. People will know whether the minister is preaching the gospel of love lovingly! There is no covering of this reality. A congregation has an uncanny sense of the real and will accept no substitutes.

VI. Conclusion

It is in these ways, then, that the ordinary occasion of the sermon holds the promise of being the saving Event of Christ.

59

Here is the fulfillment of the promise "There am I," the miracle of the Christian faith which makes all other miracles optional. For the faith is confirmed that God has chosen the foolishness of preaching as a means for His continuing work among us. To be sure, there will be many occasions when we have done all, yet our words fall to the ground. But there will be other times of great authenticity when we who have gathered in His name know He is among us, even as He promised. God has continued the Event in the foolishness of preaching that in Christ, as Abelard put it, He still "might illumine the world by His wisdom and excite it to the love of Himself."

CHAPTER THREE

The Pastorate:

INVOLVED FOR LIFE

IN 1767 THE AGING PASTOR AT
Waldsbach, a tiny village in the Vosges Mountains, came to
Strasburg, first to consult his doctor, then, his fears confirmed,
to go to the university to seek a successor. There he was told of
a young man who openly had set a strange condition for his
ministry. He would accept a pastorate only when everyone else
had turned it down. The pastorate at Waldsbach, a parish
known as "The Valley of Stone," seemed precisely to meet that
condition. And so it proved. The next April Jean Frédéric
Oberlin set out to begin his ministry at Waldsbach.

At first he thought it would take him thirty years, the first
ten, as he put it, "to learn every head in the village, making
inventory of moral, intellectual, and domestic needs of each."
Actually he was there for fifty-nine years, investing his whole
life in this one seemingly barren parish. He surrounded each
person under his care with a pastoral concern which expressed
itself in the daily time of prayer. It is said that villagers, passing his study at eleven o'clock in the morning, walked quietly,
because they knew the pastor was in prayer, remembering many
of them by name.

Yet at the same time his ministry was exceedingly practical. He pioneered in agricultural training, founded one of the first kindergartens on record, was elected to the Legion of Honor as an educator, and organized his community for welfare work.

How did all this seem to Oberlin? We have a word on that. Perhaps this was written on a weary Monday morning! But at least there was a time when he wrote, "The pastor at Waldsbach, if he tries to be what he ought to be in this vast and most burdensome parish . . . is a poor dog, a beast of burden, and a cart horse. He must do everything, watch everything, provide for everything, answer for everything. From early morning until bedtime I am occupied, hurried, crushed without being able to do one-half or one-tenth part of what ought to be done. Everything rests upon the pastor."[1] Yet, from that single parish there came a timeless witness to a ministry which had both depth of devotion and breadth of outreach. That "occupied, hurried, crushed" life bore an abundant witness.

I. A Life of Distraction and Dilution?

We have seen a rising question among us about the pastorate as a calling. The very resurgence of the theological interest often seems to have added urgency to the question. How can a man carry on a ministry which supports his intellectual and theological growth in the average parish where he is subjected to so many forces of dilution and distraction? How can any man be a minister of the Word in a setting of budgets, programs, endless promotion, petty concerns, and, of course, the ubiquitous committee? Perhaps, we are given to conclude, this is all right for the man who is willing to be a kind of active do-gooder, but how can the real encounter with God be found or shared in such a setting? From many sides have come both pleas and protests that the pastoral ministry is encumbered, making it almost impossible for a man to choose his own priorities. Especially if one wants to keep his scholarly interest, would he not be better off somewhere else?

We should fall into fallacy, however, if we were to conclude that it is only in the contemporary pastorate that these distractions are to be found. How easily we idealize times that are past, which from our perspective seem so much simpler! But we have only to read the letters of the New Testament to be reminded that those tiny fellowships of believers often were overwhelmed with personal and practical considerations. Professor John Knox has reminded us of an important fact: "We are likely to suppose that the administrative work required in a first-century church was much more simple than in a modern congregation of the same size. But this supposition is probably mistaken. When a first-century Jew or pagan decided to become a Christian, he became dependent upon a new community for the supplying of all his needs in a way which the modern Christian, at any rate within the West, can scarcely imagine. It is these practical concerns which appear again and again in the letters circulated among the churches. Visitors needed hospitality; letters of introduction must be written from one group to another; offerings must be taken for the relief of those in distress; moral aberrations had to be handled. There was hardly an aspect of the human situation, often in its petty forms, which did not find its way into the life of the early church."[2]

Nor is there really any time in the centuries which followed when the pastor was not confronted by many details which seemed digressions from his central calling. George Herbert's *The Country Parson,* written in the years immediately after the Reformation, at first seems to us, in our complex and industrial society, to reflect a ministry notably simple and single-minded. But even in that day the minister in the local parish had many responsibilities, among them to see "that all things be in good repair: as walls plastered, windows glazed, floors paved, seats whole, firm and uniform; especially that the Pulpit and Desk, and Communion Table and Font, be as they ought for those great duties that are performed in them. Secondly, that the church be swept and kept clean, without dust or cobwebs, and at great festivals strawed, and stuck with boughs and perfumed with incense."[3]

They were not without their lesser duties, too! Yet it is undeniable that the contemporary pastorate has suffered from a vast elaboration of external things. In part, it is a reflection of our culture. When ends and values become confused, men seem always to react in two ways: First, toward elaboration and multiplicity. This has happened in government, in education, in labor; in fact, in most of the common endeavors of our society. This is the era of the superstructure, the interrelated committees and councils. In this regard the parish certainly has gone along with the tendency of our age. The second reaction is accommodation. When we are not sure of our own ends we take over someone else's standard of success. In an era which places great confidence in measurement, we find it difficult to accept the truth that the Church really deals with immeasurables. So we find something we *can* measure, and the contemporary parish, which considers itself "up to date," has become a marvel of statistics and surveys and objective tests. We *are* seeking to judge our success in the church as we would judge any other institution in our society.

Sometimes it reminds one of the work of a man named Wahlstrom, as reported in our magazines. Wahlstrom is a tinkering kind of man, and a few years ago, wanting some recreation, he purchased an old bombsight and took it apart to see what made it work. When he started to put it together again, he discovered that he had some parts from other projects, and became fascinated to see how he could add these to the mechanism. This proved to be such a fascinating pastime that it became his hobby. Neighbors began to bring in parts and pieces, and Wahlstrom's mechanical ingenuity was turned to putting them to use. It has been going on for ten years now, and with a remarkable touch of genius Wahlstrom has been able to use most of the wheels, cogs, belts, and other parts which have been brought to him. The result of these endeavors is a machine which appropriately is called "Wahlstrom's Wonder." It has ten thousand parts. When he throws the switch three thousand of them begin to move. It is a marvel to behold! Wheels intermesh with wheels; lights flash, bells ring, belts from big wheels run many little wheels, and all the time the whole apparatus is revolving on a turntable. No doubt of it, there is a touch of genius in Wahlstrom! There is only one small difficulty. It doesn't do anything. It just runs. I shall not bother to spell out the parallel!

Then what is the answer? Where will preaching come to full dimension if not in the local pastorate? Both our theology and our history make clear that the local pastorate, with all its encumbrances, its distractions, and occasionally its irritations, is absolutely central in our ultimate Christian concern. The local congregation is the distinctive form of Christian fellowship. There is no koinonia in general. It is in the local congregation that the Christian preaching ministry must find its focus and its context. It is here that the incredible claim will find its fulfillment or its failure. It is here that the Event of Christ must be mediated week in and week out to the deepest needs of people.

But is it possible? Can it be real? We have heard much about the distractions of the parish and the maceration of the minister. Much of it is true, but that is not all that is true. For the pastorate has its own supports which respected and trusted can make not for the maceration but the maturation of the minister. It seems urgent to consider the pastorate in relation to three essential qualities of the preaching ministry, namely, scholarship, relevance, and authority.

II. The Scholarship of Involvement

It will be surprising to some that we begin with the pastorate as a setting for scholarship. Yet at precisely this point we need some moments of truth, even of confession. The fact of it is, if any man is looking to the pastorate to make him a scholar, the answer is clear: It will not do it. Moreover, if one is hoping that the pastorate is such a natural habitat for growing scholarly interests that it requires neither disciplines nor decisions, then obviously the hope is vain. In short, the pastorate will not make a man a scholar. In the pastoral ministry no man will float down stream to intellectual maturity. On the other hand, if the scholarly interest is real and not theoretical; if a man is ready to accept the disciplines which scholarship requires in whatever setting he may work; if a man has sufficient adaptability to recognize that not all scholarship is in the library or in the classroom, then the answer is a clear and unequivocal one: The pastorate can be a support and a stimulus to unfolding, lifelong intellectual life.

A further word seems necessary. Clearly there are many areas of scholarship which are for the specialist alone. It is the kind of knowledge which comes from years of disciplined study in depth in a single field. Such scholarship needs no testimonial. It is the very life of the theological school which in turn must be the intellectual center of the church. If this is the only kind of scholarship there is, then we must admit that in the main, the parish is not the place for it.

If, on the other hand, scholarship also means weighing lesser things against greater and making a sound value judgment; if it means the repeated recovery of the essential as against the peripheral in Christian experience; if it means finding contemporary freshness in historical realities, and making articulate the experience which marks the church as a distinctive people of

God; if further it means finding the essential meanings of the Bible by standing in the human situations in which the Biblical witness was first born, then surely the pastorate is a superlative and sensitive point where a scholar can be deeply engaged all his life.

Perhaps we should call this the scholarship of involvement. It is the kind that comes when a man carries his intellectual inquiry into the living situation. With all the criticism of the contemporary parish, I believe that a man still has sufficient freedom to establish the process of creative alternation which makes this kind of scholarship possible. Some of the most exciting experiences of the pastor come because his work makes possible engagement in the human situation, on the one hand, and withdrawal from it to contemplate its meaning, on the other. In this rhythm of action and contemplation the minister finds his own growing understanding.

In a sense, this is really the continuous conversation of the gospel with life. How many times the pastor will discover that something he has read with little understanding at the time comes to life when he is confronted by a human situation in which he must minister. Conversely, he will discover his reading taking on urgency and point because of the demands upon him in some situation in which he has been ministering. This is what I mean by the conversation which goes on within the minister's own life as a minister. This is the scholarship of involvement.

It is almost impossible to depict the depth and scope of this experience, this unending conversation of the gospel with life in the full pastoral ministry today. Here the pastor is confronted by guilt and forgiveness, estrangement and reconciliation, anxiety and assurance, the power of sin and the leap of faith that accepts salvation. Here are all the great realities affirmed in our historic Christian theology, disclosed in life, year after year, as the minister seeks to fulfill his calling. As a parish minister he is repeatedly returning to the original data upon which Christian formulations rest. If his ministry is real he is constantly confronted by the primary experiences which led the New Testament writer to say, "That which we have seen and heard we proclaim also to you."

This seems to me especially important in a generation which has restored the Biblical witness to its central position. How can the Bible become real, in the most dynamic sense, apart from the human situations from which it arose and to which it speaks? It is so clearly a word of life, addressed to life. The pastor stands at the point of encounter between the word and the situation. The witnesses of the Bible leap into life as he stands at a bedside and recalls, "When you pass through the waters I will be with you." Or what disclosure there is in some moments of personal counsel when he has shared the burden of another's guilt and remorse, and then recalls the affirmation, "If we confess our sins, he is faithful and just and will forgive our sins and cleanse us of all unrighteousness." Or with what understanding he will recall, at a time when his own inadequate efforts have proved insufficient to help another, the beautiful benediction of Paul which speaks of God "who by the power of work within us is able to do far more abundantly than all we ask or think." Are such experiences foreign to real scholarship if they thus return us to the primary data, the original situations of God's disclosures? What better teacher can one ask than a vocation in which the unending conversation actually goes on through the common duties of the pastoral calling?

Perhaps we need to be reminded that after all it was in small local fellowships that the great realities of the Christian faith first were disclosed and understood. The New Testament letters reveal this beyond dispute. The primitive church had almost every problem of human experience, from adultery to gossip, from questions of authority to the practical relief of persons in distress. The fellowship often was divided, subject to controversy, and exploited by some to whom Christian love had been extended. Yet it was in this very setting and among these people that the great Event went on. We must remember that the letters which are our source materials were written to specific churches, dealing with local problems. In the main they did not begin as open letters written to the church at large. Each was written in response to definite needs and addressed to particular questions. From these letters came the great doctrines of the Christian faith.

Look at some of those doctrines. There is "reconciliation," for example. It was to the church at Corinth that Paul wrote, "God was in Christ reconciling the world to himself and entrusting to us the message of reconciliation." To which one might well reply, "The church at Corinth? That wasn't much to bank on." The letter itself was written in response to some plaguing and often petty questions. Divisions had arisen about eating meat which had been offered to idols and about women wearing veils or speaking in meeting. There was open competition as to which of them possessed the greatest gift in the ecstatic meetings. Even among so few believers there was clear evidence of opposition to Paul, and the real possibility that other factions would take over the church at Corinth altogether. Many of us would have counted the situation hopeless. Nevertheless it was to this church and these people that Paul patiently proclaimed that "God was in Christ reconciling the world unto himself." Imagine!

Dr. Goodspeed has written of this, "It has been said that Paul's letters take the roof off the early Christian meeting places and let us look inside, and this is particularly true of the letters to Corinth. In them we see Paul as a great and understanding teacher patiently taking up the most commonplace and trivial matters in a way so searching and profound that before he has finished he has worked out some enduring Christian principle of Christian living that can never be outgrown."[4] Thus was conserved the witness to the meaning of reconciliation which had come to us in Jesus Christ. Talk about an earthen vessel! But talk about a treasure!

Or consider another great word "grace." In what setting did men discover its meaning? Again, it was in local fellowship, often struggling to maintain a foothold against the tides of opposition and persecution. Even a glance at a concordance will reveal that while the word "grace" is recorded only fifteen times in the whole Biblical record up to the Book of Acts, from that point on it appears at least a hundred times. It was to Romans that Paul wrote, "Through him we have obtained access to this grace in which we stand." But even these words of such tremendous importance were addressed to a church in Rome to which by Paul's own word only the humble had been called. In all honesty, if most of us had tried to be pastor to such a church, we would have been tempted to go to the proper authority and suggest that probably our work was done, and we should look for another field. But it was precisely to this unpromising, divided, and often petty fellowship that the meaning of grace was entrusted.

Or once more, look at that cherished word "agape." The 13th chapter of I Corinthians reads to us like a poem. But that is our conditioning. The original setting was not exactly poetic. Ordinary people were bickering in an ordinary way about gifts within the church. Imagine bickering about spiritual gifts! Only you do not have to imagine it, you know it is true. To that very group Paul wrote the 13th chapter of I Corinthians. It was to such churches that the word of John the Elder was circulated: "See what love the Father has given us, that we should be called children of God: and so we are." If it is unbelievable now, it must have been even more so then! But this was no future promise; this was a present fact—"so we are."

Our concern, however, is not history, but the urgent present. It would seem that we have an important recovery to make, a recognition that the great realities of our faith still must be found where the profound often meets the petty. The contemporary pastor, kindled by his theological inquiry, must go on to say with Walt Whitman, "I must be afoot with my vision." We must move beyond the idea that when a man goes into the pastorate he thereby has chosen against scholarly interests. To the contrary!

This insight came to us from P. T. Forsyth over half a century ago in his series which, by common agreement, stand as one of the towering contributions to the Lyman Beecher Lectures. Surely here was a scholarly man in every sense of the word, giving authority to a confession which he included at the outset of his lectures. "There was a time," he said, "when I was interested in the first degree with purely scientific criticisms . . . but fortunately for me . . . I could not treat the matter as an academic quest. I was kept close to practical conditions. I was in a relation of life, duty, and responsibility for others. I could not contemplate conclusions without asking how they would affect these people, and my word to them, in doubt, debt, grief, or repentance. . . . And they were people in the press and care of life. They could not give their minds to such critical questions. If they had had the time, they had not the training . . . yet there were Christian matters which men must decide for themselves, trained or not."[5] Not only in our practical ministry to persons but in the actual vitality of our Christian scholarship our loss would be immeasurable if the scholarly mind were not found in the pastorate.

III. Dialogue with Life

But now let us make the truth flow the other way, as it were, and consider how the pastorate contributes to *relevance* in preaching. If, as we have contended, the gospel is a word not only definitely given but specifically addressed, it must follow that the pastorate speaks to us constantly of the needs to be addressed. It is revealing to note that the figures which Jesus used in his parables often have one mark in common; namely, that they connote active, transforming power at work. So when he spoke of light he implied an action against darkness. When the figure was leaven it was to be at work in the whole loaf; when the figure was salt it was to redeem that without savor. The figures which Jesus used leave us no conclusion but that the Christian word is an applied truth. It is something to be communicated, to be put to work, to be brought to bear upon specific conditions of human life. Only as preaching really does this, can it fulfill its claim and calling. All this is obvious, but it needs to be said again that we may see that the pastoral responsibilities are not necessarily distraction from preaching, but a constantly stimulating context for it.

There is a temptation to become a closed guild of those who are in the theological inquiry. We have our own words, we share distinctive categories of thought, and we begin our discussions with one another on certain assumptions. All this is necessary and basically good. But there is no full Christian ministry until we break out of that special circle and impart that saving truth to those involved in life, even those who will not understand the words and categories we use. If men ask us for bread, as they certainly do, will we give them a quotation from the latest theological treatise? When Jesus commended the cup of cold water given in his name he must have meant the real thing and not the formula H_2O.

In short, as pastors, we are physicians. When a discovery is made in medicine there is an urgency to see that the new knowledge be put into practical form and made available, not only because our intellectual enquiry seeks it, but because lives may be saved by it. When the polio vaccine was discovered the next urgency was to make it available and distributed, for all the time polio was active and lives were threatened. In a sense, our theological truth has that same kind of urgency and for the same kind of reason. Repeatedly we need to break in to the theological discussion and say, "Meanwhile, back in the parish . . ." For we are engaged in a constant and unremitting struggle to redeem human lives. Despair and anxiety, sin and pride, do not suspend operations. All the time they are relentlessly at work. So a knowledge of the saving truth of the gospel among the few who can engage in full theological pursuit obviously is not enough, and was never meant to be enough, most of all by those engaged in it. Someone *must* make it available to those who will never understand theological categories.

This admittedly seems to be laboring the obvious. But I am seeking here to make the point that just as there is a vocation of theological inquiry which has its own disciplines, so there is a vocation of communication, with *its* discipline and its skills, and together they are a partnership in the gospel. Someone must "care enough to send the very best," as a familiar advertisement has it. To say that God's disclosure is His work, is not to take away the urgency of our doing all we can to give Him clear channel. To find the way to preach the Word so that it can be grasped, to strive for simplicity that makes it as clear as possible, to find the form that makes it obtainable and retainable, to relate it to the already felt needs of those who hear, and to add to it the warmth of one's own confession of faith—these are a part of a special vocation, something to which a man is called and for which he diligently prepares himself all his life.

In a sense, this is speaking a word for the specific function of the minister *to* the church. I am wholly in sympathy with the current emphasis upon the ministry of the laity. It is indeed an urgent restoration of the New Testament meaning of the church and its ministry. But granted this ministry of the laity there still remains a ministry *to* the laity, which must not be downgraded. Often these days able men who stand at the threshold of decision wonder whether they cannot minister better as laymen. To which there is one answer: that depends upon one's gifts and calling. For with all our concern for the ministry of the laity, there still is the specific ministry in the church, in my judgment, which accepts the disciplines of preaching, teaching, support, and the pastoral care of those who, in their lay ministries, will seek to penetrate our culture.

It is reported that Carlyle came home one day from a sermon which seemed to him labored and repetitious. He said to his mother that if ever he were asked to preach he would go into the pulpit and say, "People, you know what you ought to do, now go do it!" After a moment his mother replied with a gentle chiding, "Aye, lad, but would you tell them how to do it?"

Not only to help them learn how to do it, but constantly to remind them why, and in whose name—this is certainly a vocation in itself, a call to be a pastor to the ministers. In this responsibility a man grows in the ability to make the gospel relevant, available, and understandable. We urgently need men who will accept the full dimension of that responsibility!

IV. The Living Authority

Having considered the contribution of the pastorate to two qualities of preaching—scholarship and relevance—we consider finally the matter of authority as it emerges in the pastorate. It is an insight to be kept. It is a timeless reminder that while real authority is theologically grounded, its practical validation lies at last in the witness of a whole life. Today, as always, authority comes to its fullest meaning when the Word is preached by a man who ministers faithfully in several ways to the very people to whom he preaches.

A. J. Gossip, who followed by some years Ian Maclaren in one of his pulpits, learned this truth from observation. Maclaren would say from the pulpit, "Let us be kind to one another for most of us are fighting a hard battle." But what gave authority to the word which so easily might have been a vague moralism, was the life of Maclaren himself. A. J. Gossip said that in following him in the pastorate he found "how bonnily he had lived on this dictum; heard nothing of his sermons though he was a mighty preacher, but wherever there had been a little bairnie ill in his time, twenty years after they remembered in their homes the man who spent long hours pouring out wonderful stories to hot, restless little folk, too ill to look at pictures, sick or peevish or fretted in their beds."[6] We may well protest that this kind of pastoral relationship is no longer possible in the complex and often impersonal culture in which we minister. Yet I am more and more persuaded that this note of personal awareness is the need of the contemporary pastorate. In the long run it brings a note of authority to what we say, the personal confirmation of any theological argument we can present.

It is also at this point that the contemporary minister may well temper his familiar protest against the multiplicity of his pastoral responsibilities. To be sure they are excessive. There are too many committees, and often too many programs and projects. But one thing is important to see. No man ceases to be a pastor when he is in these relationships. He cannot complain that he has no time to be a *pastor* because he is too much engaged in the committees, the boards, the administrative duties, and the various demands upon his time. There is encounter, real encounter, even in a committee meeting, if a man knows his calling as pastor. Some of the laymen in a church will know their minister best by the relationship with him across the table in a board meeting. Here they will know his real intent, the integrity of his word, his priorities. He could not cease to be pastor even if he chose. I am convinced that the man who really preaches the Word of God on Sunday thereby carries with him a distinctive relationship wherever he goes into the other duties of the week. He may even rebel against this. But in part this is where he finds the wholeness of his ministry. Paul said, "This one thing I do." Actually he was doing a multiplicity of things, but they all were going in the same direction and serving the same end. So to him they *were* one thing.

Suppose a man set about to cut out of the contemporary ministry all those activities which divert him from his main calling. Some present claims would go and one would be a better minister by the loss of them! But in the real showdown we would be amazed to see how much one would keep. For the answer to the minister's loss of identity in his ministry is not first of all elimination of activities, but integration. If a man can recover the sense that he is about his ministry wherever he is in touch with people, then this is not necessarily a confinement in a stereotype someone else has imposed; it may be the extension of *his* concept of the ministry into all the several responsibilities which fill his week. By the very nature of his relationship which admits him to the deeply personal places of other people's lives, he cannot be "just an administrator" or a "mere executive." In all these he is consistently a pastor working among the people of God and in this reality he finds the wholeness of his ministry.

If then the minister will accept this wholeness which underlies the activities of the contemporary pastorate, he will find two things: a new meaning in the activities which often seem burdensome, and a new authority in his preaching because to the Word proclaimed has been added the witness of a pastoral faithfulness day by day. This is the practical authority which gives meaning to a man's words.

V. *Making the Church Vital*

We shall not have brought a fitting realism to this subject if we end here. For in our desire to emphasize the living and real possibilities in the contemporary pastorate, we must not gloss over the urgent need for vigorous reordering of our church life. Urgently and earnestly we must be about the business of putting away the extraneous, and releasing the real. Our next step in our theological recovery seems to be reordering the life of the church in the light of our essential beliefs.

It seems to me that the hope for this reordering lies in a pastoral leadership which sees the problem and knows what it is about. It is my deep conviction that this is not only imperative, but possible. We have looked long enough at what the parish does to the pastor; let us look now at what the pastor can do for the parish. There is still sufficient freedom for the minister to lead a church into that release which brings reality to the koinonia and agape which are the essence of the real church. Such freedom both allows and requires certain things of us in our pastoral leadership.

One of these is that we need to make deliberate disavowal of some of the popular misconceptions of the church. Probably there was a time in our generation when we needed to harmonize Christian thought and belief with contemporary ways. The church did need to adjust to the world, its categories of thought, its new areas of knowledge, its useful skills. But that is not the primary need now. We shall lose our identity, and obscure those distinctive qualities which mark the real vitality of the church, unless we make clear those ways in which the church is different, standing off from other areas of our common life.

We will recognize anew that the church is an organism growing from within and taking on its form according to its essential nature, rather than an object formed by outside influences. This is one of the differences between a manufactured object and a growing organism. That which is manufactured takes on its form by the mold in which it is cast. It is shaped and tooled from outside; it does not grow into its form. An organism, on the other hand, has an essential nature which emerges, matures, and forms the organism. One of the things we say in our confession that the church is the Body of Christ is precisely this: that we are an organism, our form emerging from an inner, unfolding life. What we become must be determined by that inner nature more than by outward molding influences in the culture. In short, by our essence rather than by our environment. This has been caught with graphic effect by Phillips in his translation of the familiar verse in the 12th chapter of Romans, "Don't let the world around you squeeze you into its own mold, but let God remold your minds from within, so that you may prove in practice that the plan of God for you is good, meets all His demands and moves toward the goal of true maturity." This is a word spoken with precision to the contemporary pastorate. In order that we may be perfectly clear about it we sometimes must make deliberate disavowals which state what we are *not*, in order that we may have a chance to be what we really *are*.

Years ago a friend called my attention to an article in a scientific journal which dealt with the questions: What is a living organism? How do you determine the difference between that which is living and that which is inanimate? The writer said that there are essential marks of that which is living. First, sensitivity, a responsiveness to its environment; second, movement, the ability to initiate action; third, assimilation, or the capacity to take substance from the environment and make it a part of itself; and finally, reproduction, the power to reproduce itself. To read these is to find interesting parallel to the marks of vitality in the church. It is this kind of livingness which requires us to make clear that the church's form and order are determined from within and not from without.

In similar way the pastor will help bring vitality to the church when he accepts the responsibility for interpretation. By this we mean a persistent asking *why* as well as *how*. We already have spoken about the urgency of interpreting to the whole church the meaning of preaching. Why should we confine the discussion of preaching to preachers? If, as we are saying so often these days, the act of preaching involves shared encounter with those who listen, then clearly they also must have some understanding of the meaning of this repeated act of faith. But this is also true of worship and of the pastoral relationship. It even moves over, often with great effect, to the boards and committees which are so much a part of contemporary church life. Repeatedly, with wise restraint but with great faithfulness, the pastor can seek to be teacher as well as organizer, interpreter as well as promoter. In staff meetings, in committees, in boards, and certainly in those times of instruction through which people are brought into the life of the church, the pastor will seek to lead people into the knowledge of the *meaning* of the church's life. Fresh in my memory are times of real excitement—just that, excitement—when people saw for the first time the full and real meaning of what they had been doing in the repeated practices of their church. There is a great compensation for the minister in those moments when someone says to him, "I have been in the church a long time but this is the first time I really understood what we were doing here!"

When the pastor is aware of this possibility, he finds an amazing number of openings. When programs are being planned, or procedures are being worked out, there will be points at which the sensitive pastor can raise again the question of meaning. He can help the people of his church make their decisions in the light of their growing understanding of their true nature as the Body of Christ. Some in every congregation will respond when the opportunity is given and when a respect for their understanding is reflected in the pastor's way of dealing with even the ordinary decisions. The cumulative impact of this kind of teaching ministry goes a long way toward keeping the life of the church vital.

With this disavowal of the imposed patterns and the constant interpretation of our essential nature as the church goes another kind of reordering which is proving its effect in many ways. I refer to the small fellowship group. In simultaneous and spontaneous rediscovery of this kind of fellowship our churches in their corporate life are making possible deeply meaningful relationships. It is a way of expecting encounter.

Almost from the beginning of the church two concepts have been in conflict. One, of course, is that of the inclusive church which reaches out in breadth to include all who will make their profession of faith and become part of the people of God. The other is the concept of the sect, a small disciplined group setting requirements that only the most faithful can keep. It is significant to note that the New Testament concept of the church really is marked by the bringing together of *both* dimensions, the height and breadth. This concept of the church seems to set an incomparably high requirement: "Be perfect even as your Heavenly Father is perfect." Yet at the same time it says "whosoever" and is open to all who will come. This is the amazing mark of the Christian church, and it is a matchless distinction in the societies of men.

This means that the church is best understood, if it were put into a diagram, as a series of concentric circles. People stand at many distances from the center. But church life must be so ordered that wherever a man stands he is drawn by constant attraction toward the center. The movement of the life of the church must be centripetal not centrifugal. The church can include those who stand even in the outward circles of its life but it cannot be content to let them stay there, if by any kind of persuasion and attraction it can start that believer moving toward the center.

It is precisely in this ministry that the small fellowship group has such a vital contribution to make. Often it is in this kind of experience that a person starts moving toward center. Somehow through the group gathered for study, for prayer, for mutual acceptance, for support and insight, and for service, there is an unmistakable stirring in the lives of persons. This becomes another way the contemporary church moves toward vitality and reality. One of the real aspects of the small group is that it does stand off against the other movements of our culture, affirming personhood when so many things have become impersonal, expecting disclosure when so many influences mask and hide our true identity, bringing acceptance and freedom and mutuality. It is a way by which we say in local context what was affirmed so often during the war: Let the church be the church! Exactly! And that means the church on the corner, too!

VI. *Ending Up in Debt*

Through all of this you will have detected, I am sure, the definite bias of a great affection. After these years, there seems to me no greater honor that can come to a man than the invitation, "Come, be our pastor." What this offers, of course, is not a guarantee, but a tremendous possibility. It is a possibility to be involved for life, your life, the life of others, and, I believe, the life of Jesus Christ in our world. If a man gives himself fully to this he may make up his mind to one thing. In all he learns, in all the fulfillment that comes in the relationships open to him, and in the abiding sense that this is where Christ becomes most real, he will find that he does not minister nearly so much as he is ministered unto!

CHAPTER FOUR

The Word:

THIS WAY TO LIFE

THERE IS HUMOR, BUT MORE THAN HUMOR, IN the story of the little lady who was taking the grand tour of Europe. For a long time she had saved for this experience and was living every moment to the full. But when she came to Westminster Abbey she became increasingly troubled as the guide showed her through, pointing out one historical memorial after another. At last unable to stand it any longer, she burst forth, "Young man, all this is very interesting. But what I want to know is: Has anyone been saved here recently?"

As often is true, the humor points up a truth. The New Testament makes clear beyond dispute that the word given us is marked "urgent," since it is for the saving of life. The whole ministry of Christ confirmed his word that he had come to seek and save that which was lost. In one sense the very belief in the Incarnation implies that the distinctive mark of God's mighty act in Christ is not merely the disclosure of His love, but the immediacy and availability of it. In Christ God stooped to conquer with suffering love.

It is this faith which highlights the tremendous importance of the vocation of communication. The very term "gospel" connotes intimate address to human need. That is what makes it news, and, because of the human situation, good news. So the minister's calling cannot be described only in terms of intellectual inquiry into truth, important as that is. Nor is it a dialogue which takes place among theologians alone. The urgent mission of the church makes a further vocation essential, namely, that which transmits the truth we have clarified by our inquiry to lives hungry for personal fulfillment. It is not enough, therefore, simply to preach as though we are to say, Take it or leave it. It must be clear we hope they will take it, and that we count it essential to completeness of life. So we bring the witness and weight of our love toward their taking it.

Our concern then in this present thought is for pastoral preaching and its part in the fulfillment of persons. We may assume no monopoly of the concern. We are a voice crying not in the wilderness but in a bedlam. For a multitude of voices cry, This is the way, walk in it! The gospel must be heard in the high competitive bidding of many pseudo-gospels. Contemporary pulpits are many, from the advertisements which try to exploit the urge for fuller life to the ends of profit to the cynical movements which seek to harness personal drives to political ambitions. Books urged upon us in almost every corner store portray life in sensual or material terms only, or perhaps in the quiet despair of living without any essential meaning. In such a cacophony, the Christian preacher must be heard. Within the brief hour of a Sunday worship service ours is the ministry of bringing a word both authentic and discriminating which speaks to deeper levels of personality where essential motivations are rooted.

It is clear that only preaching which has this new depth dimension really can help persons find fulfillment. The superficial and vain repetition of the usual clichés clearly will not do it, and, in fact, may have the tragic effect of confirming the suspicion that we have nothing very real to say about life's actual options; or the familiar sound of the usual words may give a false sense of having heard and understood their meaning. Yet the gospel which knows the reality of decision allows us no escape from the competitive preaching which marks our age of communication. How urgent it is that we learn again the art of preaching which is personal, which is heard in the context of confidence, and which deals simply with the real options confronting every person as a person.

I. Which Way to Life?

One of the first requirements for moving on to deeper levels in preaching is to recognize the continual inner conversations going on in any life. The disclosures which come to any pastor supply ample evidence that these are unending dialogues. Preaching which takes these into full account is a way of saying to another person, "I couldn't help overhearing your conversation. May I put in a word here?" Preaching is getting into the deeply personal inner conversations with a special word entrusted to us, a word which changes the very premises with which these inner conversations begin. And if we enter into another's inner conversation the least we can do is begin with *his* subject, not ours. Those sermons which really are means of grace seem to be those which most understandingly touch upon these tensions of the inner life where the basic issues are pondered. Consider for a few moments these tensions of personality which mark every life. As preaching addresses itself to these it takes on its new dimensions of depth.

One of these, of course, is *the tension between frustration and fulfillment*. Every person is under the command *to be*. That urge to fulfillment will not be lifted out of life. It may be repressed and grow destructive; it may be diverted and run into the bizarre; or it may flow into the enduring relationships of life and find consummation. But just as energy is never destroyed but only changes form, so the drive *to be,* always is operative in any life. Yet it is repeatedly meeting frustration and this back-and-forth struggle toward fulfillment becomes the rhythm of living.

Whoever deals with human motivation discovers this tremendous life force at work. We call it by many different terms: libido, life urge, the will to live. We may differ in terms but we cannot deny the reality. Erich Fromm has said, "Life has an inner dynamism of its own; it tends to grow, to be expressed, to be lived. The more the drive is thwarted, the stronger is the drive toward destruction: the more life is realized, the less is the strength of destructiveness. Destructiveness is the outcome of unlived life."[1]

A great sense of release and fulfillment came to persons who first were caught up in the Event of Christ. The New Testament witness is clear beyond doubt at this point. Those who were "in Christ" knew that another word had been introduced into that unending dialogue between their frustration and their urge for fulfillment. They would not have expressed it in these terms, for these are the words of our culture. But they had their own ways of speaking of it. They knew and proclaimed that Christ had come in order that they might "have life and have it more abundantly." They proclaimed that "in him was life" and added that "to as many as received him gave he power to become the sons of God." So real was this difference that they could describe themselves only as "new creations." They had a way of setting their old kind of life against the new, a confession by contrast. From the New Testament days to this, the witness has been so constant and so clear that the Jerusalem Conference summed it up, "In Christ we know what God is and what through Him man may become." As Christian preachers we indeed have something to say in this inner conversation between frustration and fulfillment, and it is important to say it persuasively.

Or consider the tension between judgment and grace. That also is there, beneath even the most sophisticated exterior. The pastor will not be deceived by the appearance of indifference or the false gaiety which so often hides inner anguish. A pastor who comes to a relation of confidence with people soon goes beyond surprise on those occasions when unexpectedly he finds himself looking beneath a mask of self-sufficiency upon a life aware that it is under judgment and seeking for some means of grace. I have often thought that some ways of life we choose might be compared to a child running downhill. At first it is an exhilarating experience to sense the power of gravitation. It makes us feel free and relaxed. But the illusion changes quickly. Excitement gives way to uncertainty and uncertainty to panic, for the same power that brought excitement is about to take command and, unless someone steps in, the fall is certain. We may be sure that in any congregation there are some who approach the point of panic. What seemed freedom is about to end in fall. The inability to stop is part of the judgment and only some clear word of grace and forgiveness can stop the downward plunge. It adds a tremendous urgency to the preaching of the sermon to know that some who hear at any given time are at precisely that point in their lives.

If our pastoral relationship is real, we will look many times upon the sheer reality of judgment in human life. We will know that it is a loving judgment, the other side of grace, but it still is judgment. It is that state in which autonomy and personhood are threatened. Judgment is to live by the sensual until we become increasingly satiated and decreasingly satisfied; then we must try to increase the sensual only to discover that it accelerates the downward spiral. Judgment is to live an ever-contracting life, drawing in and trusting no one until at last we trust least

of all ourselves. It is to violate relationships until we lose the
capacity to relate. It is to hoard things not for their use or
enjoyment but because they seem essential to status and security.
It is to live by force only to discover that it merely increases the
threatening counterforce we fear. It is to see through everything until we see into nothing. It is the distorted vision, the
bound affection, the broken relationship, the servitude to ap-
petite, the point at which we live as we do, not because we
may but because we must. If the gospel has a good word to
speak to that condition, then what urgency there is in speaking
and speaking it well!

The judgment we most commonly confront in our time seems
to me to be that associated with our materialism. One of the
parables most relevant to our generation is that in which Jesus
pictured a man who had such an overflowing crop that he had
to build extra barns to store it. When his barns were built and
his crop was harvested, he went out to look upon his abundance.
But he did not say that he now would have plenty to share with
his neighbor, or even that he would have more than enough to
feed his own family. He looked at his barns and said, "Soul . . .
take your ease." This was the tragedy and that was the judgment. He was trying to get a spiritual result from a material
possession, ease of soul from abundance of things. And Jesus had
a blunt word, "Fool." It is an insight which cuts squarely across
so much of our activity.

It was this same truth which Isaiah pictured in his classic story
of the idolator who went into the woods to cut down a good
tree. When he came back he used the first portion of the
wood to build a fire to warm himself. Then he used more of it
to cook his food, for he was hungry. Thus warmed and fed, he
looked about to find some scrap of wood he had left, and being
a worshiper of idols, from one fragment he carved a small
wooden idol, then prayed that it deliver him. With telling

effect Isaiah concludes, "And the residue thereof he maketh a god."

Now there was nothing wrong in any of the uses to which this man put the wood from his tree. After all, it is necessary to be warmed and fed. That was not the judgment. The point at which life came under judgment was in the order of things. It was leaving God for the residue. This was literally a disordered life. It is striking to see how Isaiah's picture stands in stark contrast to the order which Jesus gave us in his word, "Seek first his kingdom, and all these things shall be yours as well."

This is, in fact, the disorder of a wholly secular life. Its tragedy is that it takes a part of life and makes it a way of life. It turns the goods into gods. The result is a disorder which comes under judgment because it is a denial of the First Commandment; it is having other gods before God.

There is a judgment which deeply affects persons in this materialist disorder of life. It is precisely here that the gospel of God's grace can speak to many in our time. Here again we will not be deceived by outward appearances alone. We will know how often the inward hunger for release lies just under the surface. A biographer of Pascal finds the hour of his deepest spiritual need at precisely the point of his seeming success. Of that time the biographer says, "To himself and to his friends he must have appeared well over the threshold of a dazzling career, but he was profoundly unsettled, . . . Behind his businesslike attention to business, his growing ease of manner in society, the delight of new friends, the quiet pleasure of reading Epictetus, the thrill of reading Montaigne, lay an unappeasable distaste for it all and a great weariness." In time he was to come to that hour of which his biographer concludes, "Externally Pascal was a made man and a celebrity. . . . Inwardly he was beaten to his knees looking every way for help but not greatly hoping for any. For who could give him what was not there to be given?"[2] This same need will be recognized by the preacher as he comes to bring the Word of God's grace. He has something tremendous to say to this conversation, this continual inner tension in many a life between judgment and grace.

In similar way, there is the *inner tension between anxiety and assurance*. By anxiety we mean, of course, not just the passing feelings of apprehension which accompany times of stress. Real anxiety is the feeling that the very center of life is threatened, that one's very personhood is at stake. In varying degrees it has been named as a mark of this generation. Perhaps we are not as much an age of anxiety as we have commonly stated, but the pastoral preacher often will address his sermon to the vivid disclosures of this inner struggle he sees almost daily.

Consider what anxiety really is. When I was a boy I went out in a boat on the river with my brother and decided to swim back to shore. But before I covered the full distance it was evident that I had either underestimated that distance or overestimated my strength. Still vivid is the memory of those moments when I would stop swimming and try to rest my foot on the bottom of the river, hoping I could find a place to stand. Finding none, I had no choice but to swim a little farther, then try again for a place to stand. This searching for foothold and finding none is the feeling of anxiety. It even has its Biblical description, for in the 69th Psalm there is the plea "Save me, O God! for the waters have come up to my neck . . . there is no foothold!" What unforgettable moments those are! If the preacher has a word of assurance upon which the anxious at last may stand, it is superlative news, the difference for some between life and death.

It is at precisely this point that preaching today often comes under criticism. The personal crises which bring anxiety, some feel, are too deep and too individual to be helped by preaching.

This requires a ministry of personal counseling, the kind of continuing personal meeting where trust can emerge, where counselor and counselee can work together to find the source of the problem. Preaching, some contend, actually can be dangerous in dealing with matters so deeply rooted. For it is a mark of the anxious person that he can take a word and turn it to some meaning which the preacher never intended. Or he may even take the preacher's word to gloss over the real problem, thus making it more difficult for him to be helped.

Now, beyond doubt, preaching cannot take the place of that skilled counseling which must be a part of the pastor's life. But there is a ministry of preaching which can enter into this conversation between anxiety and assurance to lead not away from counseling but toward it. Moreover, there is a supportive word which is related to all the times of anxiety we know and in the preaching encounter it can be mediated to distressed persons, giving that foothold where a man may stand long enough to engage in counseling!

In the Biblical word, there is an ultimate ground of standing which offers the only assurance to which we can hold in some of the deepest testings of our lives. For "knowing God" had a special meaning in the Biblical sense. In some uses as in Jeremiah 31:34 it really means not simply "we know" but "we know that we are known." "And no longer," says Jeremiah, "shall each man teach his neighbor and each his brother, saying, 'Know the Lord,' for they shall all know me, from the least of them to the greatest." The word "know" as used here literally means "know that we are known." It anticipates that affirmation of Paul, "Then shall I know, even as also I am known."

This is an assurance of profound significance in the awful aloneness of anxiety. The cut-offness and the sense of severed relationships are burdens of the anxious person. Surely it is a word of sustaining comfort, in the best sense of that word, to hear the assurance of the gospel that we are known. It gives hope of a future when "I shall know" but an immediate assurance of a present when "I am known." In the time of testing a man well may be thrown back upon this Biblical sense of the meaning of the knowledge of God. The Biblical assurance is like the word a father gave to a small son hesitating to make the leap into his arms at night. The boy pleaded that he could not see his father. The father replied, "But I can see you." And that is the word of assurance brought by preaching to our times of anxiety.

Once more, there is also a continual *tension between self-sufficiency and reliance*. To this, pastoral preaching addresses itself. A pastor comes to feel that judged by what it does to human life, the doctrine of self-sufficiency is our cruelest heresy. To be sure, belief in oneself is essential to the fulfillment of life. But it is not the primary belief; it is, in fact, a derived one. Just as one's emotional maturity is marked by the movement from dependence to independence and then on to interdependence, so the Christian sufficiency in maturity comes to rest at last in deliberate and grateful acceptance of unchangeable reliance upon God.

As a matter of fact, the reluctance to accept this reliance is probably our greatest source of anxiety in the contemporary culture. Many counselors seem to accept the view once widely heard that one's religion often is guilt producing because it makes a man try to live up to impossible moral standards which he believes God imposes. But there is serious question whether this really is the main source of anxiety in our culture. Far more common, it seems to me, is the guilt which comes from the belief that one ought to be self-sufficient, and the repeated discovery that he is not, in spite of his best efforts. We have been conditioned to believe that the mark of maturity is self-sufficiency. But standing by itself, that is an impossible and fallacious hope. We are predoomed to failure in it. Yet we struggle on, hoping that a little more effort will do it. We never accept the good news of our reliance. Real maturity is that which accepts at last man's proper place in the order of things as given us in Genesis. Even the old story of creation gave man dominion over all other things, but still required obedience to and reliance upon God. There is a sufficiency and a serenity in accepting at last this rightful place within God's order.

It is significant to note how many of the figures Jesus used about himself imply a continuing relation: bread, water, light, physician. All these are taken from our common life and speak of recurring needs. We can never take care of them once and for all. For the next day our need will be there and we shall need more of the same resource. It is a significant insight. There is a peace to be found when at last we renounce the false hope of a sufficiency resting in ourselves, and accept instead our rightful reliance upon God day by day. There may be some occasions when God comes to us, as the light came to Saul on the road to Damascus, a blinding, dramatic, intruding Presence. But more commonly God comes to us as the sun rises each day to dispel the darkness for that day alone with the assurance that though the night will come again, so will the morning. How much is caught up in the affirmation of the Psalmist, "He restores my soul!" The need is never ending, but, by God's grace, neither is the resource.

Here then are four continual inner tensions always in human life. To live is to experience them. They help clarify for us how real pastoral preaching brings the word into the conversation already going on. This is, in part, the meaning of the hour of preaching. It is bringing a new word, a saving word, into the dialogues of personhood.

II. Invitation to Fulfillment

The next step in our inquiry is clearly before us. We need to understand more fully what it is we have to say as Christian preachers when we get into the inner conversations of other lives. Surely the word must be distinctive, carrying the unmistakable tone of good news. We very much need to find the way to say this to our generation.

The search for a form for communicating the central meaning of God's great Event in Christ is age-old, clearly reflected in the New Testament itself. It was as though men caught up by the whole experience constantly were looking for language which would encompass and impart that experience. Whatever they used proved only partial, for the experience constantly refused to be caught in any one image, or held in any one doctrine. The language they used usually was a picture or an image which would be understood in the culture of that time.

Those images have become a cherished but special language of the community of believers. The writer of John found his picture in the idea of the sheepfold with Christ as the door: "I am the door; if anyone enters by me he will be saved, and will go in and out and find pasture." That is one way the word was introduced into the conversation. At other times it was in a more abstract way. "The Word was made flesh and dwelt among us." The central Word was put into many forms not merely one, because no attempt could be spared which would communicate it to those who needed it so much. The Event of Christ was interpreted in terms of sacrifice, of ransom, of priesthood, of Logos. To those of us in the believing community these concepts, like the shared experiences of a family told over and over, take on added meaning with each generation. But have we a way by which we can convey, as though for the first time, what the Event of Christ means? What form is faithful to the meaning and gives best promise of being understood even by those who are outside looking in?

The answer to this, for some of us, is found in the basic image of *invitation*. This seems to catch the essential elements of the

93

Christian way to the fulfillment of life. For invitation by its nature offers new relationships, and these are the very heart of the Christ Event. Invitation as the image of the gospel is grounded Biblically and summarizes the main elements, it seems to me, of that real and holy history consummated in Christ. Consider the unfolding of any invitation and see how it corresponds to the unfolding of life that leads to fulfillment, as the Christian word interprets it.

To begin, there is the element of *initiative*. A true invitation comes not by our seeking but by another's willing. We who receive the invitation are the sought. Sometimes it is a surprise, coming even from one whom we do not yet know. Then one day, there it is—an invitation that opens by another's initiative the way to a new relationship.

This so clearly corresponds to the recurring note of the Bible. We already have spoken of the way in which we depend upon God's initiative. So in the fulfillment of life, the beginning comes when we are made aware of those ways in which God addresses us to say, You are wanted. A word comes to us which opens the way to sustaining relationships, first with God, then with others, and finally with ourselves, from which the real fulfillment of life comes.

It is at this very point that the Christian news stands out against the temper of our time. It is generally assumed that if there is to be initiative it must come from us. Life is seen by many contemporaries as an unremitting struggle against the overarching indifference in which we exist. Before such indifference, we at best may enjoy the passing satisfactions of the moment, or cherish times of tenderness toward one another. But whole areas of our contemporary life assume indifference and no initiative but our own. In Tennessee Williams' play *Sweet Bird of Youth* there is a point at which a character called the Heckler steps forward center stage to speak a word which explains in part the dreary lives portrayed before us. The Heckler says, "I believe that the silence of God, the absolute speechlessness of Him, is a long, long and awful thing that the world is lost because of; I think it's yet to be broken to any man living or any man yet lived on the earth, no exceptions."[3] No invitation in that. Far from it!

Against this stands the Biblical faith, affirmed and reaffirmed in the whole witness. In clear contrast is the singing faith of Hebrews, "In many and various ways God spoke of old to our fathers by the prophets; but in these last days he has spoken to us by a Son." And what has He said? He has said, "Come!" With that word all of life begins with a new premise. Barth once said that many lives are like equations with a minus sign in front of them. God's initiative in the gospel changes the minus to a plus sign, so that the same elements and conditions in life's equation are transformed to totally new values. This is what God's initiative means, and we must preach it.

At the same time, the idea of invitation seems to me to emphasize a second element, namely, *decision*. An invitation narrows the decision to either yes or no. If the word addressing us is definite, so there must be an answer, one way or another. The vague "sometime" gives way to "now" and this so clearly is descriptive of those points of decision which come in a living Christian faith. In our preaching we must help make clear that the truth in Christ is the kind to which we must say yes or no, give assent or make denial. It allows no indefinite neutrality.

Often the pastor thinks of the people to whom he preaches regularly. Hearing such words about decision would cause many of them to say, What decision? What are you talking about, when you speak of something requiring a yes or no? If a man has to decide whether or not to buy a house, that decision we understand. Many decisions are like that. We must either take a trip or not take it, for we cannot do both. We choose one college as against another. We accept an offered position or we decline it. All of these we understand as definite decisions. To choose one option is to rule out all others.

But beside these the Christian truth seems to many of us to require no such definite choices. If there *are* decisions we seem quite capable of holding them in indefinite abeyance. Who can say how many people have been going to church for years, hearing the word about commitment and decision but never really making up their own lives about it? It leads us to realize how preaching today must clarify both the need for and the nature of decision: to trust or not to trust, to give of oneself or to go on withholding oneself, to accept identity as a Christian or to try to be many things to many people, to give the Kingdom claim over our time and substance or to give these resources to something else. There are decisions arising from God's invitation. And in our preaching we help men find fulfillment if we can make the decisions more clear and imperative.

Beyond initiative and decision, the image of invitation also includes the step of *response*. In other words, when the time comes for the appointment to which you have been invited, you must go! In a sense this always is an act of faith, a moving out upon the assumption that the invitation is trustworthy. The parallel to this in the fulfillment of the Christian life seems evident indeed. We go as far as we can to meet the word of invitation.

It is suggestive to think how Jesus had no single act of response which he required of everyone. It surely must have been a mark of his love for each person that the form of response he required seemed always commensurate with the ability of the one in need. Undoubtedly he could have healed the blind man without requiring him to wash in the pool of Siloam. But going along a path already surely familiar became the outward sign of an inward readiness. This much he could do. He could make his way once more to the pool to wash. The act in itself was not really important, but the response to which it bore testimony was essential. Or to require a man to take up the very bed on which he had been lying before he was healed must have seemed an unnecessary requirement. Yet again it was something he could do, and it too became the evidence of his acceptance of the offered forgiveness.

This, to be sure, can be corrupted to a kind of magic in which our salvation is in the act itself. Rather we receive wholeness by the response of which the outward act is only the expression. If one really has heard the invitation to fullness of life in Jesus Christ, there are some things he can do: He can make his confession, or unite with the fellowship, or make restitution to the one he has wronged, or accept a new discipline of prayer, or offer his daily work as a new kind of vocation. But in any case it is not the act that counts so much as the response to which it bears witness. It is our way of saying, I have come to keep an appointment because I believe the invitation to life is fully to be trusted.

Consider another stage of the unfolding invitation. It is a part we often overlook. It is the experience of *waiting*. Again we lay hold upon our image of invitation. When we go to keep the appointment and knock at the door to which we have been invited, there often is still a brief time of waiting for the door to be opened. We do not want to labor this picture, but it has something to say to us. It helps to explain those times when, having done all, we can only stand. And those times come to us all. When we have given the best explanation we can, we stand before their mystery. Why should there be times of waiting when it is God who has invited us? We can only say that these too require our trust. This is at least one meaning of the repeated Biblical injunction to "wait upon the Lord." But it is waiting with expectancy—that is the point! All men have times

of waiting, for life never moves in unchanging pace to its fulfillment. But even in the times when nothing seems to be happening in the affairs of faith, there can still be an expectancy, a
looking forward with hope, a sustaining belief that in the fullness of time the door will open. He who has invited will confirm
his invitation in his own time.

So the invitation accepted brings us at last to the *encounter*.
We are the reconciled, and we become the reconciling. Sometimes it is a profoundly moving experience in which we come
to this saving relation with God. We can say of the love of God
what Elizabeth said of Robert's love for her.

> . . . I who thought to sink
> Was caught up in love and taught the whole
> Of life in a new rhythm.[4]

But for most of us it is discovering the reality of the majestic
traditional confession of faith that "the end of man is to glorify
God and enjoy Him forever."

There is a paradox in this. The encounter with God in one's
life so often is recognition that He has been there all the time.
It is discovering, as those who walked to Emmaus discovered,
that He has been with us the whole way. But there is a moment
when our eyes are opened and we recognize Him. This is the
point at which, upon accepting what God always has been offering, we move into a new relation of trust, joy, and that reliance
which "throws itself upon God in life or in death" which Luther
said "alone makes a Christian man." Thus centered down in
the reconciled relationship to God, our lives find the new sufficiency and completion which is the promise of the gospel.

This comes close to our calling as preachers. It gives urgent
meaning to our pastoral preaching when we remember that
everyone, by the very nature of God's way with us, is at some
point in this unfolding invitation. Preaching can be the way by

which the initiative is disclosed, the decision made clear, the response called forth, the waiting given hope, and at last the divine encounter recognized. To me, this is an unfailingly exciting possibility, inherent within the hour of preaching. It is this invitation which we introduce into the deeper inner conversations always going on in the persons to whom we preach.

III. What Pastoral Preaching Requires

This brings us to stand once more before the preacher himself to ask what personal qualities are required of him in the kind of preaching of which we have been speaking. It was a part of the audacity of our ministry that in Protestantism we have put our reliance upon personal relationships as the chief means of mediation of God's grace. This means that the quality of those relationships is supremely important. We have to cherish those things in us which will offer clear channel to God's great invitation. There are qualities in the preacher as a person which give authenticity to his word about the way to life.

For one thing, it is clearly required that he really care for persons in particular and not just people in general. Let none of us underestimate the difficulty of doing this, and avoiding that deadening professionalism which is our occupational hazard. No small part of the discipline of the pastoral ministry is keeping that kind of caring which seeks the response of another as the sign of his salvation and not the sign of our success. Bluntly, it is not easy in the many demands of the ministry to be sure that persons remain ends and not means—means to our success, evidences of the power of our ministry rather than of the power of God to save and fulfill lives.

Some time ago a man in deep mental distress climbed out on the parapet of a high building in the downtown section of one of our cities. There he stood precariously near the edge, contemplating the jump. During several anxious hours men tried every way to draw him back from destruction. One of those who made the appeal was a minister from a nearby church who sat on the window sill and made an appeal to the man who was beyond the reach of his hand. Now how do you plead with another man for *his* life? Any of us would know how to plead for his own. The sheer instinct of survival would give us that knowledge. But to plead with another man for *his* life requires a special kind of caring, a deep concern for every man as a man. As preachers we all will have times when we feel ourselves in that same position of seeking to make the appeal with another man for his life.

At that point the real quality of our caring will become apparent. Nothing phony, professional, or assumed will do it. It is a kind of caring that never could come about by horizontal relationships alone, or even by the commandment to love our neighbor. This pastoral quality which accepts and affirms another person to whom the appeal is made is the outward sign of the minister's inward relationship to God. It seems that we cannot say that too often! Only the reconciled minister can be the reconciling preacher. And one of the evidences of our obedience to God is the love for persons in which we love where we are not loved, care where we are disregarded, and look upon each life whatever its present condition as one to whom God already has extended His great invitation. Only the man who has not tried it could count that an easy thing to do, or more exactly, to be. But it is the priceless ingredient in pastoral preaching.

Along with this is the second quality, namely, personal confession of faith. Again Drummond caught it for us when he said, "Christianity does not need more advocates, it needs more witnesses." We cannot extend the invitation of the gospel by standing outside and saying, "Go in"; we have to extend it from inside, saying, "Come in." With uncanny insight, people will know which way it is with us. Make no mistake about it, they will know. It will not be necessary to fall into that practice which easily becomes so repetitious, namely, relating our own experiences and becoming an autobiographical preacher. The personal confession is an underlying authenticity pointing not to ourselves but to the word upon which we are relying in our own lives.

Is it not true that times of real renewal in the Church often have broken through the confession and refreshing of the ministry itself? We think, for example, of Hugh Latimer as one of the Christian martyrs, a man who in the last hours of his life sought to bring courage to his comrade Ridley. But we know that it was not always so with Latimer. It is said that one day when he had preached an impressive sermon in King's Chapel, Cambridge, he was met at the foot of the pulpit stairs by another member of the academic community commonly called Little Bilney. "Father Latimer," said Bilney, "may I confess my soul to thee?" So the two of them went into a little room under the pulpit. There Bilney told Latimer of the inner struggle which had been his over a long period of time; he confessed his search for security, his hunger for assurance, and the seeming failure of a search which had been only intellectual. Then Bilney confessed that only in recent days he had found his peace in a new and utter reliance upon God who had given Himself in Christ. As he spoke, tears came to Latimer's eyes and he confessed that he, too, had been in this agony, but not yet found release. So the priesthood of all believers became real as the two men knelt and each prayed for the other. There both men came to the ultimate obedience, the surrender which is freedom.[5]

Even our concern for the reordering of parish life, urgent as it is, cannot keep us from this prior urgency. There is no reordering which can recover our identity as preachers and pastors apart from our own renewed confession. On the other hand, if our confession has reality, there are so many openings through which it can be imparted, even in the contemporary ministry. The word we preach cannot be understood, let alone preached, by one who stands on the outside, an advocate but not a witness.

Again, pastoral preaching will take on its full stature when it is marked by another quality in the preacher, namely, mature discernment. It is the insight that can distinguish and is not afraid to point out what is real and what is unreal, what is good and what is only apparently good, what is true and what is untrue, what is genuine and what is counterfeit. One way preaching can take on greater reality for those who listen is in dealing more honestly with the false alternatives which present themselves to everyone who makes the Christian decisions.

One summer driving out of the High Sierras our family was surprised to find a strange sign along the road just as we turned toward home. The sign said, "This is not the road to Fresno." This led us to speculate how busy we would be if we started labeling all roads indicating where they do not go! But undoubtedly behind this was a repeated and common mistake. This obviously was a road easily taken for the highway to Fresno! Experience posted that warning.

The Christian criticism of life often must be the other side of the word of invitation. How often the prophets of Israel had precisely this burden! There was the note of warning as well as invitation, and that same note sometimes will be heard in preaching which is faithfully pastoral. This ability to discern the real in the midst of the subtle offerings of the counterfeit is a part of the responsibility of the contemporary pulpit.

Or consider a final qualification. It is, I think, the mark of maturity to accept the necessary limitations in even the best pastoral relation. There is an anguish about being a pastor and preaching a word which we believe leads to life. For we soon discover that the most we can do is extend the invitation; we cannot compel. Somewhere in my ministry I acquired a strange connotation to the phrase of the Lord's Prayer, "Forgive us our trespasses." So often this brings to mind the picture of one man trespassing upon the personality of another! Let it be clear that I am not offering this as an exegesis of the Lord's Prayer! It is rather a reflection of some temptations with which the pastor grapples. We still find it difficult to accept the "No Trespassing" sign which God has put at the threshold of every man's life. We sometimes are restless about letting Him be finisher of our faith, as well as author of our faith.

Some years ago there appeared a play under the title *The Man Who Played God*. It is good to know it was not about a minister! For we are tempted too often to assume that role, another mark of ruinous professionalism. At best, however, the minister is like the man who introduces two people and when the introduction is made steps out to let the conversation go on between them. Pastoral preaching rests upon the willingness to make the introduction. It cannot compel the conversation. We cannot be forever eavesdropping, breaking in to make suggestions, or insisting upon the direction in which things must go. Not even Jesus compelled Nicodemus to come back and pick up the discussion again. Not even his love for the rich young ruler would allow him to run out and bring him back to see if, on second attempt, he could not be pressured to sell his goods and follow. There is strangely both an anguish and a serenity in this knowledge that as servants we are never greater than our Master.

All our lives we must carry this tension, the concern to see it through in another life and yet the knowledge that there soon comes a point when that life is beyond our reach. But then there are the surprises. Sometimes seed of the gospel seems to be winter wheat. We go along planting as best we can and yet for a long time look out upon a barren field, a winter scene. Then one day, with some strange change of climate, things begin to happen. A letter comes from someone in the congregation whom we do not know; a man walks into the office and tells us of a sermon which was decisive for him; a young couple discloses that on one crucial day they heard a word that helped them make the decision which kept the home together. These well may have been times when we thought nothing was happening!

IV. Beyond All That We Ask or Think

This leaves us standing at a place of refreshment, a faith for the busy, often distracted, sometimes harried pastor. What honor is comparable to this—that God with His infinite power seems to have stopped short the full giving of Himself, thus allowing room for an ordinary man to be mediator, to span by his faithful workaday ministry the remaining gap between a person and God who invites him! There will be sufficient days when it will come with full force that because of the word we preached—or, audaciously, Christ preached through us—men and women actually recognized the grace of God in their lives. Then trusting, they joyfully moved on to that fulfillment which God has willed for every life. That day we will know the privilege of our calling.

CHAPTER FIVE

The Imperative:

WHERE THE KINGDOM
AND THE
CULTURE MEET

THE TEMPER OF OUR TIME IS RE-
flected in an exchange which takes place between two characters in Brendan Behan's play, *The Hostage*. An older man is
telling of his part in the Irish Rebellion. As often is true, the
retelling becomes a reliving and his fervor mounts moment by
moment. At last, completely caught up in it, he turns suddenly
to a young girl in the wide-eyed group of listeners and demands,
"And where were you when the fighting was going on?" Completely taken by surprise, she recovers enough to reply, "Me?
Why I wasn't even born yet!" At which the old man turns to
the others and, with a mixture of triumph and dismay in his
voice, complains, "There you are! Excuses, always excuses!"

There is evidence enough that this kind of intensity grips
many people in our time. When the foundations have been so
shaken even our loyalties often become more than loyalties; they
become plans of salvation, and deviation is regarded as heresy.

Yet it is part of the contemporary paradox that there often

exists side by side with this intensity an amazing indifference on the part of other men. Some of us faced by catastrophic events are like the Rev. Mr. Kilvert who recorded in his diary on September 3, 1870, a day which brought decisive defeat to France, these revealing words: "The news was brought from Hereford this afternoon that MacMahon's army had been surrounded and that the Emperor himself had surrendered in person and given up his sword to the King of Prussia. What a tremendous collapse! . . . I sat next to Mrs. Bridge at dinner and we had a very merry time."[1] It would not be difficult to find many parallels in our generation. This is the paradox: intensity and indifference, side by side. Yeats seems to have described us precisely in his lines:

> Things fall apart; the center cannot hold,
> Mere anarchy is loosed upon the world,
> . . . .
> The best lack all conviction, while the worst
> Are full of passionate intensity.[2]

Now how on earth—literally on earth!—can the preacher in his pastorate live out his Christian obedience in a time when things fall apart socially, and we search for a new center? Are the issues too complex, the events too far-reaching? Yes they are. Too complex and too far-reaching for any man. But this is the preacher's tension. As a Christian preacher he is commanded, and tactical decisions must be made. Can a man be pastor and also prophet, seeing in the often perplexing events of his time, as the Biblical prophets saw in the events of their times, the disclosure of God's redemptive work? As a Christian preacher does he speak any distinctive, saving word in a social struggle so complex and often so confusing? Can the contemporary minister say what Isaiah said to his nation, "And your ears shall hear a word behind you saying, This is the way, walk in it"?

The Imperative

I. The Thrust for Righteousness

Carried as we are by those social currents which flow through our generation, every preacher today, whether he realizes it or not, has been affected by the rise of Christian movements for social righteousness. He may resist such movements or seek to be part of them; but he cannot live as though they had not come. Behind him lies a century which brought the impact of the "social gospel."

The term "social gospel" we must count unfortunate, a contradiction of terms which has brought tragic misunderstanding of its real content. Social righteousness is never an alternative gospel. The good news remains what it always has been and must be: the amazing word of God's reconciling acts toward us, and the assurance of His grace. The gospel is not a proclamation of what ought to be, but of what *is*, God's saving love. But from that reconciled relation to God must come a new thrust for reconciliation among men wherever they meet. The social gospel, so-called, came from men who faced the injustices and exploitations of their society, and insisted that while Christianity is not merely a system of ethics, it is always more and never less than that. This thrust for social righteousness C. H. Hopkins calls America's most unique contribution to the great ongoing stream of Christianity. It was, he says, basically "the reaction of Protestantism to the ethics and practices of capitalism as brought to point in the industrial situation."[3]

But, like any illumination, its light went far beyond the point of its breakthrough. Walter Rauschenbusch, whose name is so closely associated with social righteousness, "woke up," as his biographer puts it, "to discover to his own amazement that he had touched the conscience of his generation and had become a major prophet of God's righteousness to His church and nation."[4] Yes, but a prophet among many. A glance at the very titles of the Lyman Beecher Lectures reminds us of that. In 1885 Washington Gladden entitled his series "Tools and the Man" and again in 1901 "Social Salvation." In 1906 Charles R. Brown lectured on "The Social Message of Today's Pulpit." In 1917 Henry Sloane Coffin reflected the war years in his series "Preaching in a Day of Social Rebuilding." In a few decades earnest and able Christian men had come far from that first stirring, which an early member of the movement caught in his word, "It isn't enough to pray *for* a man on Sunday and prey *on* him the rest of the week."[5]

These manifest evidences of social awakening propelled many Christians into the twentieth century in the expectant belief that this was to be indeed "the Christian century," as a well-known paper reorganized in 1900 proclaimed in its new name. It seemed that an impending righteousness was about to break in. War would yield to peaceful ways of change, racial justice would prevail, and the benefits of our industrial society would be shared equitably for the welfare of all men. Some may have been dragged protesting into the twentieth century, but most Christians walked into it with an eagerness rarely known in the Christian story.

II. Appointment with Despair

What followed is a story often and well told. We were barely into our century before our time of troubles began. The "Christian century" was only fourteen years old when World War I broke with its unspeakable horror. It was eighteen when the first Marxist Revolution was successful, thirty-nine when World War II came like a returning nightmare, more terrifying than the first. By mid-century we stood looking back on decades strewn with catastrophe, appalled and still unbelieving that in this first half of our century more people had died from war, and the causes attributable to war, than in any comparable period in the history of man. We indeed had come to our appointment with despair.

For many of us in the ministry today this is not history alone; it is biography. In our social concern, we could have appropriated Francis Thompson's classic words and made them a brief biography.

> Up vistaed hopes I sped;
> And shot, precipitated,
> Adown Titanic glooms of chasmèd fears.[6]

Yet in the midst of our own times of despair we had to minister to congregations and seek to keep the pulpit socially sensitive.

Recently I took some time to review the sermons preached from my first pastorate on through the years. This, I might add, is not an altogether heartening experience! Yet it was interesting to be reminded of the issues reflected in the sermons of one pastor living through the last twenty-five years. At first there were those issues centering around the dislocation and discouragements of the depression, and the attempts to support programs which offered alleviation and recovery. Then there were the problems of impending war, our nation's decision whether to stay aloof or to enter. Underlying these were the decisions of personal pacifism. At the same time, practical questions of aid and relief for neutral but distressed peoples were before us. When the war broke on that terrible Sunday afternoon, the anguish of disrupted families and the thousand fevers and fears of conflict had to be set in the perspective of a faith in the sovereignty of God. In time there emerged the compulsion to postwar planning, a movement which probably was as much an outlet for our frustration as a practical contribution to the future. But at least we felt we were doing something for peace. The years since the war have brought us a succession of issues far too long to mention: the imperatives of racial justice,

McCarthyism and the challenge to basic freedoms, aid to under-privileged areas of the world, the needs of displaced persons, universal military training, the attempts to impose the loyalty oath on persons and institutions, fair employment practices, the support of the United Nations, religious tolerance, the control of alcohol in our culture, nuclear testing. My word! What issue hasn't come up for decision? And with this were occasional local involvements in new forms of city government or the election of members to a school board.

Now in retrospect there is the haunting question: Did such preaching really do any good? Was it really within the pastor's province to deal with these matters? Many preachers seem to have concluded that such things are really not our business. Pastors trying to preach Sunday by Sunday and to touch upon the points where the Kingdom and the culture conflict will understand the common Biblical protest of the prophet that he really was not meant for such a task! Timidity and uncertainty form an easy coalition.

Not many years ago, when science and our inherited faith seemed in conflict, we sometimes spoke of "astronomical intimidation." By this we meant that the new universe we were discovering seemed overwhelming and brought us to a sense of insignificance. Today, grappling with inexorable events, we seem to face another kind of challenge, namely, historical intimidation. It is the haunting feeling that history moves impartially with a blind force which makes even our best ethical protests often impotent and insignificant. Man seems to have been taken off his escalator going *up* (if man ever *really* believed he was on one) and been put on another going *down*. We indeed have had our appointment with despair.

III. The Imperatives of Maturity

Yet the appointment has been kept and I believe we have found our way through. Is not the notable theological recovery in our time both the result of and the answer to that despair? Confronted by the appalling power of social evils we *had* to find new and deeper meanings in our faith—or else! Stern realities confronted our hopes for social righteousness. The corrections of maturity have been required of us. As mid-century came on, we knew with painful urgency the meaning of *crisis* as against steady evolutionary development in our societies. We stood once more before the irrefutable evidence that sin was in every human endeavor and achievement, even our best. We saw that the love of neighbor was possible only as man's second love, derived from a prior love of God. We finally accepted the hard truth that Christian social responsibility requires difficult choices between power structures, and any one of these choices holds compromise and pretension. Yet choose we must.

Faced with these realities we have been thrown back upon deeper levels of our faith. In our social relationships we came to understand anew the meaning of our sin and God's grace, our pride and God's humbling, our limitation and God's greatness, our despair and God's sovereign word of hope. In short, we have begun again to think theologically and in social matters to find our imperatives anew. Yet the basic and timeless affirmations, both theological and ethical, have come to us. There is a new dimension in them. Theology has had to listen as well as to speak, listen to the very voices of concern and conscience which spoke of social righteousness. It is not mere chance that many young men most interested in theology in our generation are also most involved in redemptive movements in social situations.

Now it seems urgent upon us to understand more clearly how a man can be a socially responsible preacher in the average local pulpit. Surely his message must reflect the insights of the present theological resurgence and also the chastened experience of our century's social struggles. The word he preaches where the Kingdom and the culture meet must have this dimension of maturity, a new synthesis, as it were, of theology and social concern.

Voices both outside and inside the Church have been vigorous in their criticism of the Church's social ineffectiveness. We often look in vain for radical social leadership in the Church as a whole. But does this mean that the Church has failed in its mission? If the Church cannot be a political party or a social group with single purpose and strategy, or a technician in social achievements, has it then no relevance to the social revolutions of this time? Since the preacher in the local church obviously is not one skilled in political affairs or in the many technical matters which affect our contemporary societies, has he no real function in the movements for social justice? Obviously we believe that he does have an imperative vocation in these matters, and our search now is for those distinctive contributions to social righteousness which we make as preachers.

In this chastened mid-century the socially responsible preacher must speak for those basic moral imperatives which are an extension of the central event of Christ. This will bring certain recurring themes into his preaching. As I think of preaching in these years of social stress, I find that a few main emphases have emerged and recurred. By no stretch of the imagination can these be called a social philosophy or system. But, as a response to the social situation in the light of the gospel, they have become part of our preaching. At least five imperatives seem to emerge as the marks of our maturity.

First, *there is the imperative to acknowledge again and again the reign of God in human affairs.* In other eras this would have been laboring the obvious, an unnecessary repetition of unchallenged assumption. But not so in our time! How on earth can we proclaim God's sovereignty in a way which conveys all the implications which are in it? How easily it can be passed off as something which we accept in principle but deny in practice! Shall we define it in terms of "the moral order"? How urgently we need a language that will convey the full implication of this belief! Our secular society assumes tacitly or proclaims loudly that only human powers really count. We seem to have accepted Stalin's dictum that God is always on the side of the most legions. Yet the Biblical word stands stark against that. God's judgment has disclosed a power of righteousness greater than the right of power, for He is not mocked in human affairs.

What generation has had as many instances of moral judgment? Sometimes it is startling in its dramatic disclosure. Before World War I a young idealist in Austria wrote a book on John Hus. In the preface he said, "As I prepare this little volume for printing, I cherish the hope that it may arouse in the minds of its readers a hatred of each form of spiritual and secular tyranny." In later years, however, that same writer abandoned those social views and himself became a tyrant and a dictator. As World War II drew to its close that same man and his mistress were hanged by their heels in a square in Milan. You see, Mussolini's earlier moral protest had been closer to reality than his later cynical tyranny.

Nor is that judgment any less real when it is quiet and unheralded. In some ways the silent judgments, in the long run, become the most eloquent reminders of God's moral reign. It is a man whose roots are deep in the South, Gerald W. Johnson, who writes in *The Atlantic Monthly* of the reality of moral judgment as it is seen in the effect of racial prejudice on those who hold it. Looking at prejudice and its effects, he writes, "Acceptance of a fraud inevitably involves some deterioration of character. In that sentence is compressed the political history of the South since the reconstruction. Its exegesis is the whole corpus of William Faulkner's work, admittedly the greatest artistic achievement of the South in this century. The tale that

Faulkner tells in many volumes is that the very section in which once the concept of honor was so highly esteemed that, for even a fantastic idea of honor, men did not hesitate to sacrifice life itself, has now accepted fraud for three generations and has become, as one critic put it, 'tricky and mean.' It is a tragedy. It is a tragedy worthy of the novelist genius, a tragedy on a more epic scale."[7]

The secular distortion is that it sees no confronting Kingdom but knows only the culture. It is the very absence of conflict, the unawareness of any demanding judgment, which is our dangerous distortion. It makes our ethics false because our understanding of the basic reality of history is false. As Christian preachers it is our responsibility to make clear that this judgment is not only something to be dreaded but something to be trusted. The same faith that says, "God is not mocked," enables us, on the other hand, to proclaim, "If God be for us who can be against us?" I do not see how a contemporary Christian pulpit can avoid handling at times the word of God's moral judgment on our social iniquities and inequities.

Second, *there is the imperative word which defines social righteousness as a matter of personal obedience.* The social imperatives of the Christian rest not primarily upon the second commandment, the love of neighbor, but upon the first, the love of God. They are part of his response to Him who already has sought us in reconciliation. We cannot rest our social concern upon the hope for success or even the demand for results. We must make it a single-minded and faithful response to God's commandment in Christ to seek, to reconcile, to love.

The strength of this kind of deep personal commitment is seen in an insight which Nehru once brought in a word about Gandhi. Nehru was interpreting the secret of Gandhi's power among the people of India. He said that when Gandhi returned from South Africa he confronted the depressed classes of India with clear-cut decision. He said that they could be free *if* they would meet certain basic conditions: First, to give up voluntarily what they feared might be taken from them, even life itself if necessary, and second, to want freedom so much that each man would accept prison or die for it even though not one other would stand with him. Thus the commitment to freedom was deeply personal. It rested in a total, interior obedience not dependent upon the counting of numbers or the assurance of success. The result is written in history. These commitments became a single power which swept the country as a revolutionary social movement. But it really always was rooted in deep personal obedience.

Ever since I heard Nehru on this I have felt that our Christian social concern rests on even deeper personal obedience to God. The Biblical witness has made clear that a man must render justice, show mercy, seek reconciliation, and be under the law of love simply because he is confronted by God who requires this of him. Clearly the standard of his social righteousness is not horizontal but vertical. It is that in which a man realizes that love for the Christian is a command, nothing less, and it is absolute. If the most he can bring in response is an inch toward that total demand, nothing remains but for him to go that inch. For the test is not the degree of achievement but the integrity of the attempt. It seems to me imperative for the preacher again and again to make clear this theme, as he speaks of the social imperatives of our faith.

In a time when we have discovered so many paradoxes in the Christian faith, here is another: Though this is deeply personal, it has powerful social results. A man soon discovers, of course, that he is not the only one living out such obedience—far from it! And the courage so deeply needed for a time of social stress is really the outward sign of that inward obedience marked by a kind of abandon. We move on to our maturity when we cease asking first, What do the times require of us? Our prior question is, In such times, what does the Lord require of us?

Paul Geren, whose account of his experiences in Burma during the war remains a very sensitive document, brings out this fact in one incident in his story. He recalls an occasion when he was one of three men faced with the responsibility of helping move evacuees from one hospital ward to another. In carrying out this duty, the three stood in the doorway of the building which had been set aside for the victims of dysentery. It was far from a pleasant sight. The disease had made the air foul and the whole scene revolting. At that moment one of the men standing with Geren made a strange remark. "I am very glad at this very moment I am agnostic," he said. This, of course, reflected earlier conversations which these men had had. Geren makes clear his meaning in these words: "Since he did not believe in the love of Christ, he could leave the handling of these dysentery victims to the sweepers. Since his friend did believe in it he was not free to stand by and watch. Nor was I. . . . There is no need to call this filthiness sweet or to start enjoying it through a strange inversion. Only one thing is necessary; for love's sake, it must be done."[8]

Broadened out, this leads us to see that *the third imperative of social maturity is upon the church, namely, to be a peculiar people of God.* It must be counted a sign of health that in a generation deeply involved with the questions of community, we have rediscovered the meaning of the Church as a special kind of community, a new sense of being the people of God. But what of it? How are the distinctions to be seen, in some prerogatives and privileges or in new ethical faithfulness?

Looking over these years of pastoral experience I find it heartening to recall those times when this peculiarity of the Church in our culture broke through our usual ways of living. For, though many members would not be able to be articulate about it, there is a real and discernible sense of the differentness of the Church, the new commandment under which it lives. The pastor sees a church squirm under the requirement sometimes, but he also sees that church rise above the community at some critical points.

This was made clear in an early experience in my own pastorate. In a social situation involving race relations I had taken a personal stand which was contrary to the mores of the community, a stand which I felt was my personal obedience. Yet it seemed at first to bring very little reaction in the church. But after I had been away for a few days I found a note on my desk from the chairman of our official board, asking that I see him before I saw anyone else! When I called him he came immediately to my study and wanted to explain precisely what had happened. In my absence one of the members of the board had requested a meeting, simply suggesting that there was a matter of urgent concern, but not stating what it was. When the board came together, however, and the chairman asked for business, nothing happened. There was some little and aimless talk, but no issue! In embarrassment the chairman dismissed the meeting and then singled out the man who had requested the call. It then became evident that the original issue had been my action in the racial matter. But something happened to these men when they came to sit down as members of the Christian Church. Unexpectedly, there came an inarticulate but very real sense of a new responsibility. Here they faced one another as Christians, responsible for and to the church. They found themselves strangely bound by that responsibility. A whole new factor had come into their thinking. It was a tribute to their integrity that they accepted that new dimension. Here they were *churchmen* and as such had a new responsibility. These men of the Church strangely sensed a Lordship which required an obedience which they only partially understood, but still accepted.

That *is* in the Church, giving meaning to even our fumbling, pedestrian ways.

Recognizing this, the preacher will try to bring to his own church the meaning of Paul's affirmation, "You are a peculiar people." Our very distinction is that we are a community under orders, orders that carry ethical requirements. In a sense, the church *does* gather a chosen people, chosen not for special privilege but for special responsibility, yes, and special meaning in their community. To them much has been given and now much is required.

As Christians we often have asked the question, How can we help? But confronted by some of the imperatives as Christians we have another question: How can we help it? The answer is, We can't. Not if we are to fulfill the vocation of the Church in the world. The pastor will need to preach that, not in some general church pronouncement but in the specific church to which he ministers.

There is a fourth imperative. *It is to present faithfully the requirements of compassion.* However we may differ on the issues, we still must minister to persons. There is an utter simplicity about the story which Jesus told of the final judgment. The question was whether we had visited those who were sick and imprisoned, clothed those who were naked, given food and drink to those who were hungry. There is that intriguing note of surprise in the response of those who received a commendation of their Lord, "When did we see thee?" In the very question there is a disclosure of the spontaneous compassion which must mark the Church in a time of disruption and dislocation.

In the contemporary novel, *Episode of Sparrows*, the story is told of two sisters who remain in an area of London long after it has changed its character. As the area becomes less respectable it also becomes more populous! Into the neighborhood come scores of children. To these the sisters react in opposite ways. One of them, Olivia, looks upon the children with affection and concern. In asking her pastor what she should do for one of them, however, she receives a vague and pious answer that she should leave it to God, who after all cares for even the least. Her pastor piously reminds her that not a sparrow shall fall but God notes it. But Olivia, remembering the children around her, reacts in some indignation. "But, it isn't so," she says. "They fall all the time. We knock them down. We knock them, crush them carelessly or carefully, it doesn't matter which, and they fall. That's what humans do to humans. So, don't talk to me about God." There is a moment of silence, then suddenly she goes on. "Wait, humans to humans? Is that how it works? Someone, one person at least, is meant to see the fall and care?"[9]

It is a question which implies an answer. But Christian compassion goes far deeper. It is so much more than doing unto others as we would have them do unto us. It is moving upon life under the command, "Do unto others as God in Christ already has done unto you." It is a compassion which knows that we have received in advance, and never can repay the mercy which God has shown to us. In one sense, the very heart of Christian compassion, as well as the Christian ethic, is saying, "For the love of God, do something!" The compassion we show is our response to our neighbor in the light of God's prior relation to us. To accept the love of God in our lives is to be under the compulsion to compassion. To worship Him is to be under orders to do His work. So there is no escape from the works of compassion in a century like ours, and our preaching often must cut through considerations of expediency and power struggles to make that clear.

Finally, *the socially responsible pulpit will impart the urgency of even the limited ethical achievement.* We have looked long enough at the inevitable limitations imposed upon ethical achievements in a society filled with many involvements and compromises. We are now ready to hear the more mature word of Phillips Brooks, "There is a necessary limit to our achievement, but none to our attempt."

Geologists tell us that in the Arctic region there are evidences of luxurious tropical growth which once flourished on that area of the earth's surface. What brought about the change? How did an area in which plant life once flourished become icebound and barren? Geologists speculate that at some point in the earth's history there was a slight shift of the axis. It was a matter of only a few degrees. It did not turn the world upside down, but it did shift it on its axis, and that shift was sufficient to bring about the change in the climate evident in the geology of the region.

Often as preachers, trying to act within the relativities and compromises of our social life, we can remember the importance of even a few degrees' change in the moral axis on which our society revolves. To be sure, we will not bring the Kingdom by our efforts alone. We have recovered the hardwon knowledge that it is God's gift, the full receiving of which probably rests outside human history. But this does not relieve us for a moment from both the imperative and the importance of the limited things that can be achieved. Even a minor advance in civil rights, even a single move for the sake of racial justice, even a better foreign policy as against a worse one, can help to change the whole moral and social climate in which persons must live. If earlier decades of our century overestimated what human achievement can do, these middle decades have fallen too far to the other side, too readily assuming that if our achievement is limited, it is thereby not very important. Someone has well said that a little progress is not a dangerous thing, if you know how little it is! Again, it is at this point that the Christian imperative is distinctive. Believing ourselves under the command to be ethically obedient, we must attempt even the limited achievement which love requires.

This is to recover, then, the relation of the ultimate law of love to the immediate decisions which must be made. Clearly the *ultimate* will of God is the law of love. Usually in the *immediate* and complex decisions which must be made we cannot live by that law to the full. But this does not mark the immediate, limited decision as unimportant. It may be only a better law as against a poorer one, works of mercy for the homeless, or the outcast, or the exploited; it may mean the protection of those freedoms which have been won out of anguish and turmoil. None of these fulfills the law of love, but all of these are required by it. These may be the most we can do in any given situation, but they are also the least we can do.

Surely one great temptation we face in the local church is an unexamined assumption that social responsibility is a matter of words—speaking a word, on the one hand, and hearing it, on the other. The preacher is tempted to feel that when he has preached a prophetic sermon in a given situation he has fulfilled his part of the obligation. In short, by a kind of unspoken covenant the preacher does not expect that much will be done about it, nor does the congregation expect to do it! This is the corruption of a free pulpit. Is it not true that this kind of exercise goes on in churches which consider themselves socially aware, committed to a free discussion of social issues? Yet it is a listening without a sense of mission. It is asking: What shall we think about this? But the deeper question is not as evident: What shall we do about this?

Yet the church which accepts the Christian social imperatives with new urgency also finds a new hope. The same God who requires faithfulness of us has promised it to the full. William Allen White in his biography closes that portion written by his own hand with lines which are contemplative and poignant. He is thinking about the times in his life which were points of highest experience. One of those he counts to be the Bull Moose Convention when he saw men caught up in a great idealism, and for a time enlightened and enlivened by the experience. He recalls the look on their faces and the new tone of confidence in their voices. Then he adds, "And now they are dust, and all the visions they saw that day have dissolved. Their hopes, like shifting clouds, have blown away before the rounds of circumstance. And I wonder if it did matter much. Or is there somewhere, in the stuff that holds humanity together, some force, some conservation of spiritual energy, that saves the core of every noble hope, and gathers all men's visions some day, some way, into the reality of progress. I do not know. But I have seen the world move, under some maybe mystic influence, far enough to have the right to ask that question."[10]

But the Christian faith has had an answer to that question even before it is asked by such men in our time. We have affirmed that God is both Author and Finisher of our faith. We have learned that every human achievement comes at last to the point described by the writer of Hebrews, "These all died in faith, not having received what was promised"; but we know that it goes on to add, "since God had foreseen something better for us, that apart from us they should not be made perfect." This is our hope, the other side of the requirement which places the contemporary pulpit under an urgency to support even the relative ethical achievement.

So these imperatives of maturity seem to me to reflect the shift which has come in our mid-century. Slowly we are seeing the scale shift again until concerned men are confessing that the social imperative does not rest upon the doctrine of man, but upon the doctrine of God. It is not something that makes for the fulfillment of a man's life alone but first for the fulfillment of God's will. It is, in short, the fruit of our obedience which we must render to God to use as He will, whether in the fulfillment of our social hopes in our times, or in the preparation of the saving remnant from which shall come a new and better order.

IV. *The Pastoral Prophet*

What then of the man who must occupy this socially responsible pulpit? We need to look once more at his identity, especially in relation to this area of ministry. Over and over men have spoken of the conflict between the pastoral and the prophetic roles of the ministry. Yet after these years I have a conviction that they are not necessarily competitive, but often supportive. One distinction of the local Christian ministry is that in it a man may be at the same time pastor and prophet. In this is strength. It is an opportunity held by few other men who have social concern. Here lies the possibility of bringing a whole life to support a prophetic word. In the local ministry one may be a pastoral prophet, adding authenticity to the prophetic word by the very faithfulness of his pastoral care.

To be the kind of person who can bring the prophetic witness in a local community a man needs to find his identity in at least three basic relationships.

First, the preacher, I am persuaded, should be identified primarily with moral imperatives, rather than with partisan loyalties. Of course, this is not an easy position to maintain, but it seems to be the role of the pastoral prophet. In the power structures which make up contemporary society the preacher must represent an ethical position more than a primarily partisan interest. To be sure, this sounds aloof and even irresponsible when it is expressed in the abstract. Yet when one sees it in a ministry like that of Ernest Fremont Tittle, who for thirty years in his pulpit bore a witness of unmistakable integrity, he sees the power of this position. For a few years my ministry was in the same community as that of Dr. Tittle. Again and again there was the evidence that even those who did not agree with him could not deny a profound respect for his integrity. Here was a man who in every relationship, including the social struggle, was first "a man of God" who spoke from that prior commitment and from no other. Yet this was his strength, keeping him from the special pleading, the partisan bias, the kind of ethical gymnastics that would lead him to support a position simply because it was a power advantage and supported his side, rather than an imperative right. This distinctive identity, making partisanship a means instead of an end, is an essential of an effective prophetic ministry in our time.

Men who leave America for a time and come back speak of the way in which American audiences grow increasingly skeptical, and conditioned to look for the gimmick, the pitch, the special pleading which is thrown at them, day by day, even hour by hour, by almost every means of communication. Yet this means only that when people come to have confidence that a man actually speaks a word simply because he believes it to be part of the truth he preaches and, therefore, imperative, that word has added strength and freshness. Even in the complexity of our social struggles a man must make clear where his first and full responsibility lies: to the great ethical imperative of Christ.

Second, the pastoral prophet is always identified with the people to whom he preaches. This is highly important. It is important that he say "we" rather than "you." He must constantly make clear that he is among those to whom the word is addressed rather than merely one who addresses the word to someone else. How revealing that Jesus himself wept over the city of Jerusalem, still tied by compassion with the very people who had rejected him!

There is evidence enough that there are many personal temptations for the preacher dealing with social issues. It takes a constant and faithful discipline to be sure that what one is expressing is a moral judgment and not his own hostility. Often the ego finds some of its best openings, discovers one's vulnerable points, in the heat of controversial subjects. Almost in spite of himself, a man will discover that he is defending not a position but himself; that he is setting about not to proclaim what is right, but to show who is right! Next to the constant demand made upon the preacher by his pastoral work, dealing with social issues places the most insistent requirement upon him for a devotional life in which he repeatedly comes to terms with his own drives to egocentricity.

What we need to remember is that when we are dealing with social issues we are still engaged in a person-minded ministry. In a sense it is all a part of the redemptive calling to which a man has given himself as pastor. The concern for social issues is in part a concern for persons injured by injustice and prejudice. A man blinded by prejudice, supporting injustice, engaging in exploitation, or increasingly trusting in the materialism of our culture, is a person needing to be saved from destructive forces, a soul needing to be saved, if you will. It is *as pastors* that we must be concerned with social matters, for inevitably it is persons who bear the brunt of the social evils.

In this regard, then, the minister must see that his word is spoken in fellowship with the people to whom he ministers. He is no less pastor because he is prophet. He is, in fact, but extending his pastoral concern to a prophetic responsibility. This means that he is as ready to listen and understand, as he is to speak and guide. It means that he is prophet in the humbler settings of board meetings or committees where the practical decisions about the church are made and where, incidentally, he enjoys no such immunity as respect for the pulpit sometimes affords. It means that in his life both the pastoral and the prophetic strands are so interwoven that one is aware only of the wholeness of that ministry. It is this relationship between the pastoral and the prophetic which we now need to see as an important support rather than as a tension alone, as often has been said. The preacher can come to the controversial subjects speak ing from *within* the community of faith and giving daily evidence that he is identified with those to whom he sometimes must bring a word of judgment.

Close to this is the third fact that the pastoral prophet is identified with the whole ministry. We cannot say too strongly that there is an added authenticity that comes to the preacher *because* he has many functions, not only one. The prophet who stands at the point where the Kingdom and the culture conflict is also the man who stands with a family at the time of bereavement, or with a couple at the time a home is established, or with a distressed person passing through his times of anxiety. A man loses something when he becomes known as one who deals *only* with social imperatives. This ministry is as distorted as the man who never deals with the social aspects of the gospel. The pastor has the superb opportunity to make clear that when he speaks of the love of God it is not in general, but in particular. That adds the authentic note to the preaching which deals with social matters. It is summed up in the word a layman once spoke about his minister, "I never could understand the position he took on that issue, but I have loved him like a brother." Back of that undoubtedly lay those times when this man who now was speaking for social righteousness had proved himself a good pastor in the deeply personal relationships of a congregation.

V. *Urgent—Apply Locally*

All through this consideration of the social urgencies my mind has turned often to two kinds of men to whom these words seem closely related. The first are those pastors in local churches who want their ministry to be relevant to the social revolutions of our generation yet feel they are out of the main stream, paddling about in the backwaters while other men move nearer the center of these movements. It brings to mind earnest men who, devoted to the Church, still are greatly discouraged about its effectiveness and relevance to the issues with which we have unavoidable appointment.

But the other remembrance is of laymen and churches I have known, and the times I have seen them struggle with matters of Christian conscience. Still vivid are the occasions when men stood for freedom of the pulpit even when they radically disagreed with what was being said; times when churches rose above the racial mores of the community to cross lines they did not want to cross; other times when men on differing sides of social issues found fellowship in the family of the church and tempered their criticisms of each other; yet other times when the church, hearing of human needs, rose with a great sense of release to meet the demands of compassion; and yet again, some really dramatic hours when a local church reversed itself and discovered its own nature, giving at last real leadership in specific social decisions.

The sum of it is an abiding confidence that the pastor seeking to be socially responsible does have both obligation and opportunity. After all, our most urgent need now is not for restatement of general social principles, but the patient and faithful application to local situations. Just as in America we do not need a new Constitution, but the application of Constitutional principles to local communities, so in the Christian imperatives found in the Event of Christ we have been given sufficient understanding of the meaning of the neighbor relationship. To help bring this to concrete expression is our contemporary task, and nothing can serve the cause of social justice more widely than the coming to our pulpits of men both pastorally and prophetically responsible. The great imperatives confront us clearly marked: Urgent—apply locally. To this end God surely has laid His hand upon the pastor in his local ministry.

CHAPTER SIX

The Calling:

MATURING IN THE MINISTRY

A RECENT BIOGRAPHER OF GEORGE Whitefield, having recounted the amazing story of his influence, concludes by seeking the secret of his power. From that summary comes this insight: "His theology was not new. Men had previously heard all he had to say. They had not, however, heard it said quite in the idiom that he used. The difference was not in his technique. The difference was in the spokesman. And here seemingly is the real secret of Whitefield's attraction: the intensely confessional character of his preaching—the intensely confessional character of the man who preached."[1]

In the light of what we have seen about preaching this is no surprising conclusion. It is in fact part of a consistent witness. Generations later when Frederick W. Robertson made his impact upon Brighton, those who knew him best also found the secret of his power in the man himself. In the introduction to the published sermons Robertson's son bears similar testimony. "The subjective conditions which have mainly determined the bent of my father's genius," he says, "may, however, be briefly touched upon. . . . They seem to be three in number. Firstly, he was what he preached—true. . . . Secondly, he was entirely in earnest. . . . Thirdly, he was essentially courageous."[2] The words by themselves are impressive. But when one considers that they came from Robertson's son who knew the preacher as only a son could, they are an unforgettable insight into the character of this man.

Even these brief references serve to remind us that we cannot deal with the subject of preaching without coming at last to the more personal questions about the preacher himself. Nor will the answers of another generation necessarily speak to our condition. It is more than evident that the Christian preacher in our culture finds himself under new stresses and strains. In fact, so much has been written and said on this subject that we have a veritable concert of concern. We already have marked the complaint which appears in several variations: that the many extraneous duties of the average parish keep a minister from his main calling as mediator and preacher, that administration has made a man an executive caring for an institution rather than a pastor caring for the souls of men, that keeping up with our culture has made the minister an activist who has little acquaintance with his study, that the multitude of demands has brought the "maceration of the minister." Now we must note the effect of these things upon the man himself. It has given rise to a growing uncertainty among older men about their calling, and a disturbing reticence on the part of some younger men to choose the pastorate as the form of their ministry.

If these indeed are the most important truths about the contemporary pastorate, we need to be concerned and deeply so. For these factors help determine what kind of person the minister becomes as he matures in ministry. We often speak of the urgency of preaching the whole gospel to the whole of life. But it is also true that the Word needs a whole man if it is to come through to other men. Can the minister, then, achieve wholeness in his calling today in the midst of the fragmentizing and diverting influences which play upon him? Can he keep center when so many centrifugal forces seem to be at work? In short, how real can the minister be as a person in his relationships in the contemporary pastorate? Is the maceration inevitable, or may there be the maturation of the minister instead?

It comes down at last to the question of the degree of freedom we have. We need to know whether there is enough freedom given the minister to allow him to make some basic choices in this matter of maceration versus maturation. One matures in his ministry as he passes certain determinative crises. Perhaps the word "crisis" seems too strong. Yet there are decisions in depth, and the alternatives before a man at such times are radical. In this sense these times of testing indeed must be called crises. The way in which these decisions are made will answer whether the years bring the new energies of maturity to meet the increasing demands. Every minister, by the nature of his ministry, faces these essential testings.

I. Facing the Fundamental Alarm

First, clearly the minister must make his own peace with this very sense of audacity of which we have been speaking. It was partly this need which gave support to the theological resurgence of our generation. Men like Barth found themselves overawed, even overwhelmed, by the assumptions of their calling when the full force of its meaning hit them. In one of his earliest writings Barth faced the question of preaching. "What can it mean? It means above all that we should feel a fundamental alarm. What are you doing, you man, with the word of God upon your lips? Upon what grounds do you assume the role of mediator between heaven and earth?"[3] In some way that question waits for us in quiet moments of encounter with ourselves and our calling.

The Calling

In our structured and routine ministries we often can go a long time before such moments of fundamental alarm appear or return. A man even may be in the ministry for years before the full implication of what he is doing hits him. Yet I am convinced that underneath it all there await these moments of fundamental alarm. Sheer integrity invites them. There will be those times, often appearing unexpectedly, when the question really comes home, "Who are you, you man, with the word of God upon your lips?"

Here is an essential part of the tension within a minister. For in many ways it is a question we do not want to face. However the answer comes out, there is a burden with it. If the answer emerges a negative one, then we really have no ground for our claim; our calling becomes unreal, a masquerade, a hypocritical affair. If, on the other hand, we find by asking that there *are* grounds for the claim, then the requirement becomes in some ways an even greater burden. Who can handle it? Our alarm lies in the fact that there is no answer to the question which does not make radical requirement upon a man as a man, either to be a full minister, or to give up the ground of his meaning as a person, to the degree he has sought to find that meaning in the ministry. So, probably one reason we stay busy is the hope that we may still the alarm and put off the day when we must come face to face with it.

Sometimes we try to still the alarm by the anesthesia of activity. At this point, it seems to me, some genuine candor is required of us. In all honesty, how much of our activity, so often decried by those who want to keep reality in the ministry, is imposed and how much is chosen? To what degree are we impelled from within and to what degree are we compelled from without? Here some moments of searching honesty are required of us. For an impressive portion of our activity seems self-chosen. In the face of the fundamental alarm, it is in some ways flight to an easier alternative. For it *is* easier to promote than to pray. It *is* easier to be in one's office than in the study. It often *is* easier to serve on a committee than to face the question of one's real commitment. It may be difficult to raise a budget, but it is infinitely more difficult to raise a spirit which has been crushed by the circumstances of life, or by the relentless inner tensions which bind men.

This may prove to be only a personal confession. But even if a man's pastorate did not make so many demands upon him, he still would have to come to terms with the tendency to turn to the easier as against the more difficult parts of his work and the peripheral is easier than the essential. That problem is not a mark of our own time alone. It would be a part of the ministry in every age. And apparently it has been. It is at least interesting to note that in 1877 Phillips Brooks in his lectures was quoting an observer who noted that "a gently complaining and fatigued spirit is that in which evangelical divines are very apt to pass their days." Even so today! But who is making this fatiguing demand? More than we generally admit, or possibly more than we know, it is something we impose upon ourselves to cover some plaguing uncertainties which ought to be faced.

Or again, we sometimes try to still the essential question by a kind of hidden disclaimer. We go on proclaiming a power in the gospel but inwardly we do not really expect much to come of it. This is a serious word, but it seems too often to be true. No scene is more hollow and, in the long run, more heart-breaking than that of a church and a preacher who go on with the acts of worship and preaching, all the time having unconsciously lost any expectation that much will come of it. That indeed is the vain repetition, the ultimate cynicism, because it is only outward action without inward expectation. Or perhaps even more poignantly, the hour of preaching may go on with the congregation and the preacher each assuming that somehow the other believes it, and for their sake it must go on. My word, how much better an open disclaimer than a hidden one!

As for the preacher who makes that compromise, the end is tragically clear. He will grow increasingly windy, and decreasingly real. He may even try to cover his inward despising with a boisterous cordiality. But it will not do. He still hears on occasion the clear note of the fundamental alarm, and it is a frightening sound. In a short story called "Answer to Prayer" H. G. Wells tells of the archbishop who was bothered one night by a fretting of mind. So, as was his custom, he went into his private chapel to pray. He sank to his knees and put his hands together as he had so many times before, and began, "Oh God!" And there came from the altar a clear strong voice replying, "Yes, what is it?" They found the archbishop the next morning sprawled on the stairs. It was evident that he had died of shock. But not all death is physical or instantaneous. Yet what other end can there be but spiritual death when a man makes the false peace of inwardly disclaiming his audacious calling?

Again, some may seek to cover their vocation with the less demanding avocations. It is possible to settle down to being a religious functionary in our society, performing those little niceties which tradition has assigned to us, doing faithfully just what men expect of us without facing what God expects. There are always invocations to be given at all kinds of community occasions, bland speeches on moral and spiritual values, and committees where one vaguely represents the religious interests of the city. Of course these have their place. But not first place, by any means. And not at the expense of the original office of the minister. They are indeed avocations and options. Nothing more. Yet the comment of Whitefield about the clergy of his day still has a contemporary note: "They frequent and shine in all public places, their own pulpits excepted."[4] The man of God thus becomes a man about town, busy but not about his Father's business. He is doing those things which do not require ordination by the people of God, but only recognition by his own community.

This is not to deny the place of the minister in the necessary partnerships of a community in which he lives. It is only to say that most of these functions are being met by someone else, and often with better effect. There are many who give counsel, many who help to provide social fellowship and a place for the gathering of people together, many who contribute to the needs of relief and welfare. In these the minister gladly will share, for it is part of the church's responsibility. But there is one thing no one else will do if the minister does not do it, and that is to lead men and women into a deeper understanding of the God-relationship in their lives. His basic vocation is to be a *man* of God in the most real and mature sense of that phrase. Not even all the best avocations together can substitute for that basic responsibility.

This leaves us facing the still unanswered question: How then *does* a man live with this claim which can awaken alarm? We must find our answer in the faith which took form in the New Testament. For the answer there is a clear one, given to men in times of extreme testing, and full of promise. It is the word that the encounter which makes the man a minister brings not simply a claim upon him alone, but an offered claim also upon God. God does not require what He will not offer. It is, in short, a covenant, God's offering of Himself as well as His requiring obedience of us. So the sufficiency was never meant to be in us alone but only in Him. The call to the ministry is the call to a *covenant*. The importance of that truth is almost beyond measure. Paul caught it in those early chapters of II Corinthians which deal with the ministry of the new covenant. That covenant is still the only answer to our alarm. Those chapters of II Corinthians are filled with assurance and hope, the summary of it found in the moving words of the sixth verse of the third chapter, "Our sufficiency is from God, who has qualified us to be ministers of a new covenant." That is still the only ground of our qualification. This means quite simply that the ministry in any of its expressions is a tremendous act of faith— nothing less than that! It is a mighty act of trust which goes about this audacious business of ministry, believing where we cannot prove, but taking God's word for it.

Before we have placed undue blame upon the contemporary culture for the maceration of the minister, let us see what it can mean to quit fleeing from the full claim, and to turn at last and put our trust in this word. Then we yet may be "qualified to be ministers of a new covenant." Perhaps we shall be no less active in our ministry, but it will be the activity of assurance, not that of anxiety. We even may do many of the same things which mark the pastorate today, but they will be meaningful, taking on a new sacramental nature. At least we shall be able to bring a whole man to the proclaiming of the whole gospel.

II. Sources of Personal Renewal

If the ministry is this tremendous act of faith in God's offered sufficiency, then we move on to a further needed word, namely, that it is an act requiring almost daily renewal. For as the demands recur again and again, so must our acts of reliance become part of our way of life. But where are those sources of renewal by which the minister, so often feeling driven and distracted, finds his recovery? Without them the minister learns the truth in Jeremiah's words about his own generation, "My people . . . have gone from mountain to hill and forgotten their resting place."

In his book *Pleasant Valley* Louis Bromfield in telling his story of reclaiming a farm in Ohio, includes an episode which can be a parable for us. One day it was pointed out to Bromfield that in a section of the farm known as the Ferguson Place there was clear evidence of a spring which once had flowed there. Yet at some forgotten time it had run dry and no one knew why.

This lost spring, however, soon was forgotten on the assumption that nothing could be done about it. Instead they set about the scientific reclaiming and cultivation of the farm itself. On a little plateau near the very top of the hill they put in hay and wheat to be grown in rotation. On the steep slope below the plateau, where once the water had run in torrents, carrying off the topsoil and leaving bare gullies, they planted bluegrass and white clover. Farther down, in the old orchard, they put in a thick sod of grass and, between the trees, berry bushes which never were to be cultivated.

One morning after this reclaiming had been going on for three years, a superintendent came to Bromfield and asked him to come again to the Ferguson Place. There at the old spot, bubbling from the ground, was a new spring with a three-inch stream of clear, cold water. Bromfield explains, "From somewhere down underground a vein of water had suddenly forced itself up through the soil of the pasture. . . . We had come to the place and anchored the soil above and covered the bare earth in winter with cover crops and turned much of the land back to sod so that the falling rain no longer ran off the high hill above but sank into the earth to accumulate deep in the strata of the underlying sandstone. And so as the underground reservoir grew, the accumulated water at last reached the level where on this April the old spring was reborn, gushing out from under the walnut trees as it had done when the first settler came upon it. That spring has never failed since."[5]

There is an insight in this for us. That freshness and renewal in the ministry which is the expressed concern of so many pastors rarely comes when it is sought as an end in itself. Such renewal must be the by-product of faithful cultivation and conscientious care in important areas of our total ministry. In one sense, however, this is our hope. For the very cultivations which make a man a good minister of the gospel also contribute to his renewal as a person.

One of the most important of these, of course, is the reserved times of study so essential to a sustained ministry. The issue is nothing less than the freshness of one's whole ministry year after year. The times of study included in the minister's schedule cannot be simply the preparation for the next sermon. That kind of study, important as it is, often carries away the topsoil and we frantically have to haul in enough to grow the next sermon! But the habit of study, built into the minister's life, is a means of filling in reservoirs from which freshness and reality will flow.

But this kind of word needs no further testimony in the minds of most of us. We do not need to be convinced. The real question is the practical one: Is it possible? This is precisely the concern. Several times we have reflected the mood of the contemporary pastor that his work does not allow him time to maintain his intellectual life. Is it inevitable that the reservoirs shall run dry because a man is constantly draining his resources and never replenishing them?

The most one can do here is bear a personal witness. If the minister extemporizes and takes what time he can find for his study then those times appear with less and less regularity. But if one gets his priority clear and sets about the business of building his study into a way of life then it is still possible, and doubly important. That importance is not only for the minister himself but also for the church which catches the seriousness with which the preacher comes to the time of preaching. When the members of a congregation know that a man reserves his time for study, the very habit of doing it faithfully is in itself a witness.

The only way we can approach this matter of possibility is in the preacher himself. As we have said, study is one of the most demanding parts of any man's ministry. We are less than realistic if we think that real study is less demanding than the other things we do, an escape from the labors of our office. Moreover, there never will be a time when a man can study because nothing else is required of him at that moment. He comes to his study because he has made a *choice*, a definite decision, a deliberate reservation of that time at the cost of ruling out some other demands. Phillips Brooks once said that he never sat down to write a sermon without thinking of the calls that should be made, nor did he ever go out calling without thinking of the sermon waiting to be written. We may as well make up our minds to live with that tension. There is no resolution of it. The only way we live with it at all is to recognize that without choice, without planning, without deliberate and conscientious reservation of time there will be no consistent study in the contemporary minister's life. But with this planning and with this choice it is still possible and doubly rewarding. That choice is still open to us in the contemporary ministry. It remains for us to take up our option.

Surely it is possible for a pastor just as he states his office hours to state his study hours too. It helps to begin by stating his availability. So he can say that to be available to those who wish to see him the minister has reserved specific hours for personal conferences. Not that people will come only at those times! Many deliberately will avoid precisely those hours. But it is the means of first making clear that he is always available to those who need him. Then having made this clear, the preacher can go on to say that to sustain the pulpit ministry, the hours of a specified time in the morning have been reserved as far as possible for study. To be sure, this will not guarantee unbroken hours. Far from it. Again and again a man will be called from his study, but he can go back to it. It makes clear the seriousness of his preparation and at the same time bears witness to the congregation about the first claim of the function of preaching. In itself this is one of the ways by which expectancy can be increased, and the whole congregation can be helped to lift their estimate of the place of the preaching ministry. If the pastor will make up his mind first, and then, in a quiet but consistent way, become educator of the congregation to whom he preaches, the contemporary minister can keep his study times and thus help fill the reservoir from which the water of life must flow.

This possibility remains one of the most exciting aspects of the minister's calling. Here is that alternation which makes the pastorate a place of growing and not of frustration. After many years a man will still discover that one of the most exciting times in his ministry is the hour when he closes the door to his study to read, to meditate, to seek for understanding. It is an hour which has only one counterpart to it in excitement, namely, that in which he opens the door again to walk out refreshed and possessed of new insight to face the realities of human life with which he must grapple as a minister. That alternation, that going in and coming out, can be vastly rewarding, the pulsation of a living ministry.

Needless to say, the minister's devotional life is another part of the cultivation which keeps freshness in the ministry. Many people will be surprised to learn how often the minister finds his devotional life difficult. But he does. Partly it is because in theological education he has had to move through the critical analysis of his religious beliefs and practices to find more mature basis for them. Often it takes him years to find his way clear through. Partly devotion becomes difficult because one tends to develop an immunity through the very familiarity which comes from dealing daily with sacred things. Partly it is because he tends to expect more of himself as a minister and often is surprised at his own human limitations. For these reasons and others, one does not move close to center in any ministers' gathering without finding this concern for a deeper devotional life very near the surface.

Yet here we must recognize that the hunger itself is significant. It is an old principle that we do not hunger for that which we have not tasted. Nor would we be seeking if we had not known ourselves to be found. The hunger of the minister for more reality in his personal devotions is testimony, it seems to me, to the fact that God really is at work in that man's life. It actually shows that something is going down into the deeper inner reservoirs of his personal life. Paradoxically, he may come from his own devotions all the more aware of his need, but all the more prepared to meet the real needs of the people to whom he ministers. No explaining that, but no denying it either!

In this as at few points we see the wholeness and involvement of the pastor's life. Of his prayer the minister surely will agree with Evelyn Underhill, "It means that when we come down again to our own particular case that my spiritual life is not something specialized and intense; a fenced off devotional patch rather difficult to cultivate, and needing to be sheltered from the cold winds of the outer world. Nor is it an alternative to my outward, practical life. On the contrary it is the very source of that quality and purpose which makes my practical life worth while."[6]

As we mature in ministry two notes tend to become dominant in prayer, emphases which seem clearly our response to the daily demands of our calling.

One is the note of reliance upon God's acceptance. As persons we do not ask always to know, but we do need to be known. In a sense, the minister's prayer will be the daily acceptance of the grace and sufficiency promised in the New Testament,

The Calling

God's side of the covenant which qualifies us to be ministers in the first place. Included in this is the assurance that we are known even when we do not know. How often in the reserved times of devotion the pastor will rest back upon this assurance. This was an evident part of the experience of Bonhoeffer expressed in poetic and moving words written in prison. Here he confesses the strange contradiction between what he appears to be and what inwardly he knows he is. So he puts it into searching lines:

Who am I? They often tell me
I stepped from my cell's confinement
calmly, cheerfully, firmly,
like a squire from his country house.

Who am I? They often tell me
I used to speak to my warders
freely and friendly and clearly,
as though it were mine to command.

Who am I? They also tell me
I bore the days of misfortune
equably, smilingly, proudly,
like one accustomed to sin.

Am I then really that which other men tell of?
or am I only what I myself know of myself?
Restless, longing and sick, like a bird in a cage,
struggling for breath, as though hands were compressing my throat,
yearning for colors, for flowers, for the voices of birds,
thirsting in expectation of great events,
powerlessly trembling for friends at an infinite distance,
weary and empty at praying, at thinking, at making,
faint, and ready to say farewell to it all.

Who am I? This or the other?
Am I one person today and tomorrow another?
Am I both at once? a hypocrite before others,

and before myself a contemptible woebegone weakling?
Or is it something within me still like a beaten army
fleeing in disorder from victory already achieved?

Who am I? They mock me, these lonely questions of mine.
Whoever I am, Thou knowest, O God, I am Thine![7]

Yes, that is the only security and the only sufficiency. With mounting experience this tremendous fact is recognized more and more in prayer. And it becomes enough. We are enabled through it.

The other note of devotion is increasing and unceasing intercession. When one really is involved for life, as must be true when the pastorate is real, intercession becomes both an inevitable expression and a welcome release of concern. The pastoral prayer on Sunday morning becomes only the outward expression of a continuous inward intercession born of the daily contacts of a pastor. Or conversely the minister's devotion becomes but the extension of the pastoral prayer, an extension carried on in quiet and private expression. We know that in the lives of men like Oberlin and Bosworth intercession increasingly became the center of their prayer.

This note has been included in our discussion of the sources of renewal for the minister because paradoxically that is precisely where it belongs. It is the only faithful way to describe our experience. Yet it must not bring a calculating, self-regarding motive into prayer of intercession. That, of course, is the quickest way to lose the reality of it. One cannot intercede for others because of what it will do for him! But at the same time one cannot disregard the weight of testimony which says that in intercession the intercessor finds renewal. How many have spoken of this with a note of surprise! To such a paradox we can only say, "Come and see." Let a man consistently, faithfully, and lovingly lift before God those for whom he has concern and he will discover how much he is lifted by it. It is one of the most intimate confirmations of the truth that in losing his life a man finds it. So intercession, with the acceptance of the assurance that in God we are known, becomes the dialogue of maturity in a minister's devotional life.

But full inquiry requires us to see another source of renewal sometimes overlooked because it is so basic. The fact is that the very relationships to which a minister comes by his calling are by nature *renewing relationships*. This simply means that a man who comes with a growing sense of his own identity and is faithful in his pastoral responsibility thereby finds his life renewed, even restored by the very encounter to which these responsibilities lead.

The minister often may wonder at an experience which commonly comes to him. Sometimes when he is weary with the stresses of his work he goes out to be with people, perhaps in the hospital, perhaps in a home, or in some relationship where he really is minister far beyond the casual social relationship. The result often is that he comes back renewed and refreshed. The more real his ministry the more his own renewal. He has been giving of himself yet he returns with more than he took with him. This is the experience of most of us. Many have found this at the very center of their calling.

How shall we account for it? Encounter! Reflection seems to suggest that the renewal comes from the reality of the encounter which waits for a man in the nature of his work. It is in part an encounter with other persons. When all our shortcomings have been weighed, and the several complaints which come in hours of weariness have been heard, the pastoral relation can be one of the most real in human experience. It moves straight into the primary relationships of life. And when it is real it carries its own renewal. When a man is really accepting his distinctive responsibility as a pastor he has cut through our cultural conditioning to basic human relations. In spite of all the changes which have come that is still true. The minister meets people at the points which are most real in any life, whether it is in time of trouble or in joy, in disappointment or in fulfillment. The pastor enters the circle of a family, or is accepted into another's life at precisely those hours when men experience the great universals which make us one human family. In that encounter the minister finds his own life taking on new dimension and depth.

But the encounter, in a real sense, is far more than the human encounter. Within the very pastoral relationships the minister is in the position of seeing One at work "able to do far more abundantly than all we ask or think." Again and again he sees results of his ministry which simply cannot be explained as the sum total of his own efforts, as the influence of one person upon another, or even of the combined efforts of those with whom he is working. Perhaps he will go to a home where tragedy has come, asking himself with much anxiety what he can do. Once there he may seem to do very little, except to be there, faithful in his relationship to those who need him. But he will discover that a work of grace has come about, that he can speak of "that which we have seen and heard." He will see embittered persons temper their bitterness with forgiveness. He will see the alienated really seek reconciliation. He will see frightened and fearful men and women move into an amazing courage as they come to the next testing. He will observe men who have everything, yet come to hunger for some realities of faith which they have missed; he will see these same men led along to a new kind of hunger, strangely more fulfilling than their satisfaction. How could any man see these things come about without finding himself humbled yet tremendously lifted as he actually sees something beyond himself at work? Clearly a Power beyond himself is moving in the deep places of life.

The Calling

There are those days when the pastor will go home lost in wonder, love, and praise that of all men he was called to impart this good word of God's saving grace. He will be awed by the awareness that actually he has entered, at least for a time, the succession of mediators of God's grace. He has seen something which was not merely "back there" or will come "someday" but is here now! That very recognition renews the man who would minister.

One more question arises here in our discussion of personal renewal. What of the minister's relation to his family? For some this admittedly is one of the stresses because they feel the tension between the demands of the church and their responsibilities to their families. Can a man be minister to a whole congregation and still be fair to his own family? Many men have asked this question. It is a real one, but we should not presuppose that it leads to a negative answer.

To be sure, if a man is faithful in his pastoral care he will find the time other men give to their families often not available to him. But is the test of responsible family life really quantitative or qualitative? There seems serious question whether the issue is really between being a good pastor, on the one hand, or being a responsible husband and father, on the other. It is more probable that the same characteristics which enable a man to have vital relationships to his congregation also will bring a quality to the loving relationships of his family. In either case, the question really is not how much *time* a man gives to one or the other but how much of *himself* he gives. There are families where having more time does not solve the problem, but only increases it!

In the last analysis the test does seem primarily qualitative. And there are qualities which the life of a pastor can bring to a home which will help to compensate for the undeniable fact that he probably will have less time with his family than some other men. When one considers all that comes to the minister's family by their relationships to the church, and the degree to which the minister's wife, if she chooses, can share her husband's work; when one considers further the cultural opportunities which usually are available to the minister's family; when one weighs still further the opportunity often afforded to meet people from all over the world who can give a pastor's home perspective, then it seems that the privileges of a pastor's family are infinitely greater than the deprivations.

But still there is the question: Is the family a source of renewal for the minister in his work? As any sound family relationship is a renewal for those in it, so the pastor's family must help to restore perspective and the understanding so essential to his ministry. There is nothing like a family to build a man up or to cut him down to size, according to his need—absolutely nothing!

III. Keeping Relationships Real

This brings us to one of the most essential concerns which face the pastor in our culture, namely, that of keeping personal relationships real. There is no authority or power given us which can guarantee that the pastoral relationship in a particular church will achieve its full reality. All that can be offered to any man is an opportunity, an opportunity which gives him the benefit of the doubt. That opportunity seems to be real, for men and women genuinely want to have a pastor in the full sense of the word. But the potential will be realized only by faithful and mature cultivation of sound human relationships.

The fact is that the church *can* become a kind of perpetual masquerade party. Everything is on the surface, and everyone is playing a role. Such relationships may go on for years without ever coming to the essential qualities of acceptance and forgiveness and the loving of persons as they are. Just as we put on our Sunday clothes to go to church, so many people put on a kind of Sunday personality especially tailored for that occasion. Small wonder that a minister grows restless and feels irrelevant in such a setting! There are problems to be overcome if the pastoral relationship is to break through this masquerade and become real. The minister usually needs to overcome some preconceived ideas already held by others. He will be cast in many a role not because that is what he really is but because people have come to expect him to be certain things to them. In the eyes of some he will be a judge, in the eyes of others a moralist. For others he will be cast in the role of a kind of magician whose prayers somehow have special evocative powers. He also will be looked upon as a sentimentalist whose work is to arouse Sunday by Sunday a combination of nostalgia and reverie. He will be looked upon, moreover, as a man who automatically gets behind anything for the good of the community without asking the question whether it really is the greatest good. In short, he will be all things to all men and nothing to himself—if he will let it happen. But to see that this does *not* happen is one of his first responsibilities, not to himself alone but to his essential calling. It is not his function to play a role, as we too commonly say, but to be a person, someone real representing a gospel which is real. And the very discovery that the pastor is real, a man who has his own identity grounded in a distinctive relationship to God and to people, will call out a grateful response from those to whom he ministers. In short, a pastor is not meant to be all things to all men but *one* thing to all men, namely, a minister who brings the saving event of Jesus Christ to their lives with naturalness and freedom and times of joy.

When is the pastoral relationship real? How is it distinguished from that of the physician or a friend or a loved one in the family circle? Granted that it has some qualities in common with all of these, there are ways in which it is distinctive, even unique. When someone says of another, "He is my pastor," he has given expression to a relationship which cannot exist in any other way. What then are its marks?

Certainly it will have the note of quiet, loving acceptance. To be sure, most meaningful personal relationships must have this, but in the pastoral there must be an expression of the deepest acceptance of all, that which God has offered us in the gospel of Jesus Christ. Because of that acceptance any person must feel that in the pastor he has found one to whom he can disclose himself, his needs, his fears, his real hopes, his failures, and those hungers which few men would understand. In this relationship with his pastor a man must know that he does not have to strive for acceptance; he receives that acceptance in advance. He can literally "rest assured" in it. By offering another this kind of acceptance, the pastor actually has helped him begin to experience the essential meaning of the gospel, for that kind of acceptance is very near the heart of the good news. For the old masquerade party there is now substituted another kind of invitation, "Come as you are."

Moreover, the pastor will obviously share the depth relationships of other lives, those basic emotions which mark us as persons. When the ministry is real the pastor soon finds abundant clinical experience to show that the essential emotional and spiritual needs of every person are the same. A man may hold a high position in our culture or a low one. He still must love and be loved, must have hope to which he can hold, must learn the meaning of trust, must find a sustaining sufficiency as a person, and must seek reconciliation when he finds himself cut off from others. Without these no life can know fulfillment. There are no substitutes. No quantity of superficial achievements or possessions at last can add up to replace a single one of these basic relationships. Here the minister offers encounter on the intimate levels of life. When by his trustworthiness the pastor has fulfilled the potential of his office, he can provide a partnership of saving significance to those who claim it.

The pastoral relation has these qualities, but more. For the real distinction is that all these personal relationships are continuous with the God-relationship of anyone's life. It is the constant prayer of the pastor that he may offer to a man or a woman a confidence through which the real dialogue of life can go on. In those living situations where God confronts men the pastor stands with them as interpreter, intercessor, priest, and mediator.

Strange, is it not, that in the deepest realities of life we seem always to stand at least one person away from their full possession? Mediation is written deep into all of life. Love may be, as Henry Drummond proclaimed, the greatest thing in the world, but we shall never love until someone first loves us. The resources of healing are vast and theoretically applicable to every person, but they wait for the physician to relate them to the need. We have knowledge which illumines minds and gives power to those who possess it, but millions wait for a teacher who can help mediate that knowledge to them. So in the deepest realities where God grants to men the knowledge of Himself there is still "the person gap"—that point at which it seems someone must step in to bridge the distance between the need and the resource, the person and One who seeks him. The universal priesthood of all believers paradoxically often has been interpreted to mean denial not only of special priesthood, but all priesthood. To the contrary, it makes both the need and the possibility universal. All men need someone to be their priest both in the ordinary and critical times of life, to complete the triangle of fellowship in which God becomes known. At precisely this point there is a distinctive and discernible function which we call the pastoral relationship.

But again, can it be real? Can we break through the imposed patterns, the caricatures, the masquerades, the minor roles we play? Yes, I think we can. Even today with all the forces at work in the modern church, I think we can. There is no trick, no device, no slick technique. At last analysis, the pastoral relationship becomes real as the pastor himself is first real as a person. What is required is a genuine being in the minister himself. Without this, not all the hoarded prerogatives or borrowed skills can bring that pastoral relationship to fulfillment.

But precisely here is the superlative opportunity afforded the minister. The very complexity of the pastorate against which he often rebels is also his opportunity. For it means that the minister relates to people at many points, not just one. It is not in the pulpit alone nor in the group relationship nor in the time of counseling nor in a visit in the home nor in a board meeting. It is none of these by itself, but all of these things together which serve to disclose whether a man is real or not, whether he can be trusted with life's great intimacies, and whether he is all that the word "pastor" implies. If these contacts disclose that kind of man, then the fulfillment of the pastoral relationship is to be found even in our time, and deeply cherished by those who find it.

IV. To Whom Does the Minister Belong?

We face at last the question of a minister's belonging. There must be some ultimate devotion, an accountability by which at last his life must be judged.

Sociology has added some words to our vocabulary recently. We commonly speak of two kinds of person, the "other directed" and the "inner directed." The mark of the age, we are told, is the rise of the other-directed person. We do not act

we react. We do not initiate we imitate. But in the minister's
life there is an experience which must transcend both these
categories. In a sense his life is an inner-directed one, but it is
directed by Another. We cannot understand this calling of ours,
so alien in much of our culture and speaking a foreign language
in much of our modern vocabulary, without seeing that this
Other-directedness is an unchanging part of the minister's life.
Stumble though he may, he still tries to walk at the command
of One who has called him to covenant. Waver though he will,
he knows himself a man seeking to live the discipline of obedience in his own vocation.

There are words like a mirror in the 15th chapter of Jeremiah,
a passage which really discloses a deep place in the life of the
prophet. It seems to him that God has not come through on
the promises. And he is stating again his credentials along with
his question. He is reminding God of the evidences of his prophetic obedience. Included in that description of the prophet's
life are these words he addressed to God: "I sat alone because
thy hand was upon me." Here is that strange and alien note of
a life reserved and set aside for obedience to a deep inner call.
Is that really true? Fantasy or reality, which is it? It is bound to
be one or the other. Do we really sit alone because His hand
is upon us? Surely that does not describe active, involved, com-
munity-minded ministers! Yet His hand *is* upon us. We cannot
understand our call apart from it. In the Word given to preach
which is not ours to determine but to which we must be faithful, His hand is upon us. In the very nature of the Church
which has been called to be a people of God and not merely a
social club to be led along the ways we choose, His hand is
upon us. In the restlessness which will not allow us to be less
than full ministers, His hand again is upon us. We indeed often
sit alone reserved for a special ministry among men. Like Jeremiah we may complain at times. But more often we are over-

whelmed by the burden of that privilege, and the privilege of that burden. The mark of our maturity at last is to confess with Bonhoeffer,

> Who am I? They mock me, these lonely questions of mine.
> Whoever I am, Thou knowest, O God, I am Thine!

NOTES

Chapter One. The Claim: Incredible, but Inescapable

1. Spofford A. Brooke (ed.), *Life and Letters of Robertson* (New York: Harper & Brothers, 1903), p. 259.

2. Quoted in H. L. Mencken, *Introduction to Ibsen's Plays*, Modern Library (New York: Random House, Inc.,   ), p. xiv.

3. Henry Seidel Canby, "Footnotes to 1949," in *Saturday Review*, Vol. 32, p. 176.

4. Willard L. Sperry, *Reality in Worship* (New York: The Macmillan Company, 1925), pp. 163, 165.

5. Quoted in John Baillie, *A Diary of Readings* (New York: Charles Scribner's Sons, 1955), p. 137.

6. Quoted in Francis G. Peabody, *Reminiscences of Present-day Saints* (Boston: Houghton, Mifflin Co., 1927), p. 169.

7. A. J. Gossip, *From the Edge of the Crowd* (Edinburgh: T. & T. Clark, 1924), p. 199.

8. *Expositor's Bible*, "The Gospel of St. John," I (New York: A. C. Armstrong and Son, 1905), p. 113.

9. Emil Brunner, *Man in Revolt* (New York: Charles Scribner's Sons, 1939), p. 494.

10. Richard E. Byrd, *Alone* (New York: G. P. Putnam's Sons, 1938), pp. 290-91.

11. Ernie Pyle, daily newspaper column.

12. Stephen Vincent Benét, *John Brown's Body* (New York: Doubleday & Co., Inc., 1929), p. 213.

13. Emil Brunner, *Revelation and Reason* (Philadelphia: The Westminster Press, 1946), p. 6.

14. Reinhold Niebuhr, *Pious and Secular America* (New York: Charles Scribner's Sons, 1958), p. 2.

Chapter Two. The Sermon: Something Out of the Ordinary

1. Emil Brunner, *Revelation and Reason* (Philadelphia: Westminster Press, 1946), p. 142.

2. Heb. 4:2.

3. J. N. Grou, *The School of Jesus Christ* (English translation, 1932), p. 216.

4. Thomas à Kempis, *Imitation of Christ*, Bk. One, Chap. One, par. 3.

5. Hugh Martin (ed.), *Christian Social Reformers of the Nineteenth Century* (New York: George H. Doran, 1927), p. 55.

6. *Saturday Review*, July 25, 1959, p. 22.

7. J. B. Priestley, *George Meredith* (New York: The Macmillan Company, 1926), p. 168.

8. Stephen Vincent Benét, *Western Star* (New York: Holt, Rinehart & Winston, 1943), p. 4.

9. Ernest Mortimer, *Blaise Pascal* (New York: Harper & Brothers, 1959), p. 44.

10. William Plomer (ed.), *Kilvert's Diary* (New York: The Macmillan Company, 1947), pp. 84, 85.

11. Quoted in Hugh Thompson Kerr, *Preaching in the Early Church* (Westwood, N. J.: Fleming H. Revell Company, 1942), p. 179.

Chapter Three. The Pastorate: Involved for Life

1. Marshall Dawson, *Oberlin: A Protestant Saint* (Chicago: Willett, Clark & Co., 1934), p. 109.

2. Quoted in H. Richard Niebuhr and Daniel D. Williams (eds.), *The Ministry in Historical Perspectives* (New York: Harper & Brothers, 1956), p. 12.

3. *Ibid.*, p. 152.

4. *The Short Bible*, An American Translation (Chicago: University of Chicago Press, 1933), p. 298.

5. P. T. Forsyth, *Positive Preaching and the Modern Mind* (New York: George H. Doran Co., 1907), p. 281.

6. A. J. Gossip, *From the Edge of the Crowd* (Edinburgh: T. & T. Clark, 1924), p. 33.

Chapter Four. The Word: This Way to Life

1. Eric Fromm, *Escape from Freedom* (New York: Holt, Rinehart & Winston, Inc., 1941), pp. 183-84.

2. Ernest Mortimer, *Blaise Pascal* (New York: Harper & Brothers, 1959), p. 120.

3. Tennessee Williams, *Sweet Bird of Youth*, Act II, Scene 2.

4. Elizabeth Barrett Browning, *Sonnets to the Portuguese*, VI.

5. F. W. Boreham, *A Bunch of Everlastings* (Nashville: Abingdon Press, 1920), pp. 57-59.

Notes

Chapter Five. The Imperative: Where the Kingdom and the Culture Meet

1. William Plomer (ed.), *Kilvert's Diary*, 1870-1879 (New York: The Macmillan Company, 1947), p. 79.
2. William Butler Yeats, "The Second Coming," from Oscar Williams, ed., *Little Treasury of Great Poetry* (Charles Scribner's Sons, 1947), p. 450.
3. C. H. Hopkins, *The Rise of the Social Gospel in American Protestantism* (New Haven: Yale University Press, 1940), pp. 3, 319.
4. D. R. Sharpe, *Walter Rauschenbusch* (New York: The Macmillan Company, 1942), p. xii.
5. C. H. Hopkins, *The Rise of the Social Gospel in American Protestantism* (New Haven: Yale University Press, 1940), p. 85.
6. Francis Thompson, "The Hound of Heaven."
7. *The Atlantic Monthly*, July, 1960, p. 30.
8. Paul Geren, *Burma Diary* (New York: Harper & Brothers, 1943), pp. 51, 52.
9. Rumer Godden, *An Episode of Sparrows* (New York: Viking Press, 1955), p. 208.
10. *The Autobiography of William Allen White* (New York: The Macmillan Company, 1946), p. 627.

Chapter Six. The Calling: Maturing in the Ministry

1. Stuart Clark Henry, *George Whitefield: Wayfaring Witness* (Nashville: Abingdon Press, 1957), p. 178.
2. Frederick W. Robertson, *Sermons* (First Series) (London: Kegan Paul, Trench, Trubner & Co., 1907), pp. xiv-xv.
3. Karl Barth, *The Word of God and the Word of Man* (New York: Harper & Brothers, 1928), p. 125.
4. Stuart Clark Henry, *George Whitefield: Wayfaring Witness* (Nashville: Abingdon Press, 1957), p. 43.
5. Louis Bromfield, *Pleasant Valley* (New York: Harper & Brothers, 1937), pp. 286-89.
6. Evelyn Underhill, *The Spiritual Life* (London: Hodder & Stoughton, 1937), p. 28.
7. Dietrich Bonhoeffer, *The Cost of Discipleship* (New York: The Macmillan Company, 1959), p. 15.

Biblical References

Page	Line	Reference	Page	Line	Reference
22	21-23	Ps. 103:2	68	18-19	1 John 1:9
22	24-25	Lk. 2:9 (AV)	68	22-24	Eph. 3:20
22	26-27	2 Cor. 5:19 (AV)	69	13-14	2 Cor. 5:19
22	28-29	Rev. 21:1, 2	70	12-13	Rom. 5:2
25	20-22	Heb. 1:1	70	30-31	1 John 3:1
27	15	2 Cor. 5:19 (AV)	76	7-8	Phil. 3:13
28	3-4	Lk. 4:18	78	13-17	Rom. 12:2
28	8-9	Ps. 139:6 (AV)	87	20-21	Luke 12:19
29	12	Lk. 24:31	88	1-2	Isa. 44:17 (AV)
29	19	Phil. 2:7	88	10-11	Matt. 6:33
29	25	2 Cor. 5:18	89	25-27	Ps. 69:1-2
36	8-9	Eph. 3:20	90	25-27	Jer. 31:34
37	4-5	1 Sam. 3:19	90	29	1 Cor. 13:12 (AV)
40	6-7	2 Cor. 4:13	93	17-18	John 10:9
40	24	Matt. 18:20	95	9-11	Heb. 1:1
41	25	1 Cor. 11:25	106	30-31	Isa. 30-21
45	4-5	Heb. 4:2	122	16-19	Heb. 11:13, 39
45	7	Phil. 1:5	135	2-3	2 Cor. 3:6
46	25-26	2 Cor. 5:14	135	27-29	Jer. 50:6 (AV)
68	5-6	1 John 1:3	144	12-13	Eph. 3:20
68	14-15	Isa. 43:2	151	18-19	Jer. 15:17

156

Index

Abelard, 60
Activity in pastorate, 131
Adams, Maude, 54
Administration and pastoral care, 75-76
Agape, 70
Anxiety, 89-91
Authority in preaching, 74-76
Avocations and their danger, 133

Baillie, John, 41
Barth, Karl, 95, 130
Beecher Lectures, 108
Behan, Brendan, 105
Belonging, minister's, 150
Benét, Stephen Vincent, 32
Biblical preaching, 42
Bonhoeffer, Dietrich, 141
Boswell and Johnson, 48
Bromfield, Louis, 135
Brooks, Phillips, 23, 53, 120, 132, 138
Brunner, Emil, 25, 33, 38
Byrd, Richard E., 27-28

Call, obedience to, 151
Carlyle, Thomas, 74
Chrysostom, John, 59

Church
  as body of christ, 78
  its concentric circles, 80
  recovery of vitality, 77-80
Ciardi, John, 50
Claim of preacher, 18-19
Communion service, 41
Compassion, 118-119
Congregation in preaching experience, 45
Covenant of ministry, 134

Death Valley, 51
Decision, 95
Despair, appointment with, 108
Devotional life, 139
Disclaimer, hidden, 132
Dods, Marcus, 25
Drummond, Henry, 55, 149

Emotion in the sermon, 54-55
Encounter, 98, 143
Episode of Sparrows, 118
Event of Christ, 25-31, 85
Expectancy in preaching, 39-40

Family of minister, 145
Fellowship groups, 80

157

Index

Forsyth, P. T., 71
Freedom of minister, 130
Freedom of the pew, 46
Fromm, Erich, 85
Fulfillment of person, 84
Fundamental alarm of ministry, 130

Gandhi, 114-115
Geren, Paul, 116
Goodspeed, Edgar J., 69
Gossip, A. J., 24, 75
Grace, 70
Grau, J. N., 47

Herbert, George, 63
History and faith, 110
Hopkins, C. H., 107
Hus, John, 113

Identification in sermon, 52
Identities of preacher, incomplete, 20-21
Illustration, in the sermon, 57-58
Intercessory prayer, 142
Interest in the sermon, 50-51
Invitation in the gospel, 94

Johnson, Gerald W., 113
Judgment, 86-87, 113

Kilvert's Diary, 57, 106
Knowing God, 90-91
Knox, John, 63

Laity, ministry of, 73
Language of the sermon, 55-57
Latimer, Hugh, 101
Luther, Martin, 98

"Maceration of the minister," 129
Maclaren, Ian, 75
Materialism, 87
Maturity, imperatives of, 110
Mediation, 149
Meredith, George, 55
Milner, Isaac, 48

Minister, stereotypes, 147
Mussolini, on John Hus, 113

Nehru, on Gandhi, 114-115
Newman, John Henry, 41
"News," its meaning in Gospel, 34
Niebuhr, Reinhold, 35

Obedience, 114-115
Oberlin, Jean Frederic, 61-62

Pascal, on Montaigne, 57, 88
Pastoral preaching, 83-92, 99-104
Pastorate, marks of contemporary, 12, 148-150
Pew in preaching, 42-43
Preaching
    Biblical grounds of, 22, 68
    its distractions, 62
    its expected results, 46-47
    its false standards, 64
    its partnership, 49
    relevance of, 71-72
Proclamation, 53
Prophetic ministry, 123-126
Pyle, Ernie, 31

Rauschenbusch, Walter, 107
Reconciliation, 69
Reign of God in human affairs, 112-113
Relationships
    keeping real, 146
    renewing, 143
Reliance on God's acceptance, 128
Remembrance and preaching, 41
Response, 96-97
Responsible pulpit, 119-121
Revelation, the general, 24
Robertson, Frederick W., 17, 128

Scholarship in the pastorate, 66-67
Secularism
    distortion of, 114
    its disorder, 87-88
    its resistance to preaching, 31

Index

Self-sufficiency, 91-92
Sensibility of preacher, 44
Social gospel, 107
Social imperatives, 112-122
Social issues in preaching, 107
Social righteousness and personal obedience, 114
Sources of Personal Renewal, 135
Sperry, Willard, 21
Structure in the sermon, 53-54
Study in pastorate, 137

Temptations of prophetic ministry, 124-125
Tensions in modern life, 84-92
Theological terms, 72
Thomas à Kempis, 47
Thompson, Francis, 109
Tittle, Ernest Fremont, 123

Underhill, Evelyn, 140
Urgency of limited achievement, 119

Vocation of communication, 73

"Wahlstrom's Wonder," 64-65
Waiting upon God, 97-98
Wells, H. G., 133
White, William Allen, 121-122
Whitefield, George, 128, 133
Whitman, Walt, 71
Wilberforce, William, 48
Will of God, 121
Williams, Tennessee, 94-95
Wolfe, Thomas, 19
Wordsworth, William, 57
Worship, essential elements, 38-39

Yeats, W. B., 106